The

Akita

An Owner's Guide To

A HAPPY HEALTHY PET

Howell Book House

Howell Book House
A Simon & Schuster Macmillan Company
1633 Broadway
New York, NY 10019

Library of Congress Cataloging-in-Publication Data
Bouyet, Barbara.
Akitas / Barbara Bouyet.
p. cm. — (An owner's guide to a happy healthy pet)
Includes bibliographical references.

ISBN 0-87605-491-2

1. Akita dogs. I. Title. II. Series.
SF429.A65B69 1996   96-8888
636.7'3—dc20   CIP

Manufactured in the United States of America
10 9 8 7 6 5 4 3 2 1

Series Director: Dominique DeVito
Series Assistant Director: Ariel Cannon
Book Design: Michele Laseau
Cover Design: Iris Jeromnimon
Illustration: Jeff Yesh and Ryan Oldfather
Photography:
  Cover and puppy by Paulette Braun/Pets by Paulette
  Joan Balzarini: 96
  Mary Bloom: 96, 136, 145
  Barbara Bouyet: 8, 15, 17, 20, 59, 60, 61, 62
  Paulette Braun/Pets by Paulette: 11, 36–37, 39, 44, 50, 69, 96
  Buckinghamhill American Cocker Spaniels: 148
  Sian Cox: 18, 21, 23, 26, 48, 79, 134
  Dr. Ian Dunbar: 98, 101, 103, 111, 116–117, 122, 123, 127
  Steve Eltinge: 12, 33, 38, 41, 43, 63, 67
  Dan Lyons: 96
  Cathy Merrithew: 129
  Scott McKiernan/Zuma: 30
  Liz Palika: 133
  Susan Rezy: 96–97
  Judith Strom: 5, 7, 24, 45, 53, 96, 107, 110, 128, 130, 135, 137, 139, 140, 144, 149, 150
  Toni Tucker: 27
  Faith Uridel: 2–3, 10, 64, 73
  Jean Wentworth: 22
Production Team: Kathleen Caulfield, Vic Peterson, Christina Van Camp, and John Carroll

Contents

Welcome

to the

World

of the

part one

Akita

External Features of the Akita

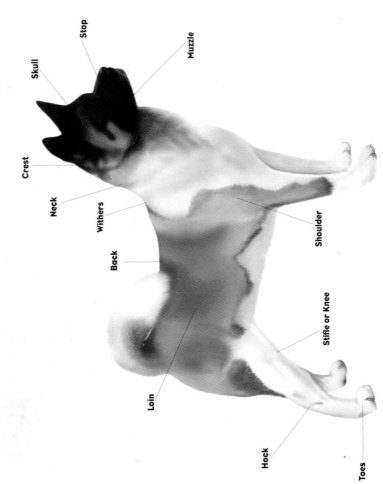

Skull

Stop

Muzzle

Crest

Neck

Withers

Back

Shoulder

Loin

Stifle or Knee

Hock

Toes

chapter 1

What
Is an
Akita?

Chances are, at some time you've seen an Akita puppy resembling a bear cub, or perhaps you've met an adult, with his imposing look of strength and power. Intrigued by his impressive appearance and proud attitude, you wonder (and are told):

"What type of dog is he?"

"He's an Akita, pronounced *ahh-KEE-tah.*"

"He looks just like a bear."

"They are used to hunt bear in their native Japan."

"Is he friendly?"

"Yes, but not demonstrative with strangers."

"Does he need a lot of room to run?"

5

"He needs exercise, as we all do, but he can live in an apartment."

What is this dog that attracts so much attention? Is he a dog for everyone? Will he fit into a family with small children? Is he very active? Does he like other dogs? Are Akitas easy to train? The answers are, "yes," and "no." "*Yes*," if you are willing to spend time socializing and training your Akita, meeting the challenges of this breed's intellect and ingenuity. "*No*," if you have a schedule already stretched to capacity.

WHAT IS A BREED STANDARD?

A breed standard—a detailed description of an individual breed—is meant to portray the *ideal* specimen of that breed. This includes ideal structure, temperament, gait, type—all aspects of the dog. Because the standard describes an ideal specimen, it isn't based on any particular dog. It is a concept against which judges compare actual dogs and breeders strive to produce dogs. At a dog show, the dog that wins is the one that comes closest, in the judge's opinion, to the standard for its breed. Breed standards are written by the breed parent clubs, the national organizations formed to oversee the well-being of the breed. They are voted on and approved by the members of the parent clubs.

As a puppy, the Akita resembles a huggy-bear cub, but he gains nearly 85 pounds during the first year of growth. With judicious but firm handling as the puppy grows into a powerful adult, you will have a devoted companion and enthusiastic guardian of home and family.

A mature Akita will have stand-up ears and a tail. The bearlike head and thick tail are hallmarks of the breed, but the infinite variety of colors and patterns makes each dog unique.

Japanese or American?

The Akita evolved in Japan through centuries of breeding to Japanese "standards." Standards are a written concept of the ideal dog for the breed, though no dog may actually reach such perfection. A breed standard details the general appearance, characteristics such as head, eyes, ears, tail, forequarters, hindquarters, topline, body proportions, gait and color. The parent breed club formulates the standard. As the breed develops, the standard is revised and expanded to reflect improvements.

In 1960 the Akita Club of America, Inc. (ACA) was formed to represent the breed as parent club in this country. The ACA was responsible for maintaining the stud book, an accurate chronicle of breeding records, and of writing a breed standard for the American Akita.

*American Akitas
are larger-boned
than their
Japanese
counterparts*

The Standard in Review

The standard for the Akita in America was designed to bring uniformity to the breed—to shape a disparate group of imported Akitas into a breed with consistent type and soundness. The American Kennel Club approved and accepted the current breed standard on April 4, 1973, and with this recognition, the stud books and the door closed on Japanese imports.

The closing of the registry caused two divergent breeds to occur between Japan and the United States. As the Japanese continued to refine and restore their Akitas, the gap widened. The closed registry barred American breeders from pursuing the same goals as the Japanese and the rest is history, as they say.

In 1992, the AKC reached an accord with the Japan Kennel Club and the stud books were reopened, allowing imported Akitas to be registered and entered in AKC shows. The differences between American and Japanese Akita standards were evident with the arrival of the first imports. Among dog show enthusiasts, the differences give supporters an opportunity for many hours of heated debate, but for the purposes of this book we will deal with the American Akita.

If you have a photo or other facsimile of an adult Akita in front of you, this section will be easy to follow (see the drawing on page 4).

Describing the Akita

The Akita is a Spitz breed, one of the "Northern dogs," which makes him a cousin to the Alaskan Malamute, Chow Chow, Siberian Husky and others. Characteristic of Northern breeds is the prominent skull, wedge-shaped head, small pricked ears, dense undercoats and powerful jaws.

Heavy bone, strong muscles, and a large bearlike head emphasize the Akita's **general appearance** as a powerful, fearless and proud dog. The thick, curled tail

enhances the perception of a well-balanced dog. The head, which is the hallmark of the breed, is in balance with the body; the tail is large enough to counterbalance the bearlike head. The Akita's intrepid spirit and regal bearing announce his presence.

The **head** is massive in appearance, free of wrinkles, with a broad flat skull between the wide-set ears. The correct head evokes an awareness of this breed's power and size. Look for the unmistakable triangles in a

The wedge-shaped head, prick ears and dense undercoat of the Akita are characteristic of Northern Spitz breeds.

correct Akita head: the overall wedge shape of the head is triangular looking at the face and as seen from under the jaw. The small eyes and ears are triangular as well. The pronounced cheeks, especially in males, add to the overall effect of size and width.

The standard lists "faults" and "disqualifications." Translated, they mean undesirable problems that occur in the breed. A fault is unattractive but a disqualification means banishment from the showring. *A narrow or snipey head is a fault.*

Eyes are dark brown, deep-set, with tight, triangular-shaped rims. A broad, black **nose** (liver is acceptable only in the white Akita) and wide **muzzle** enhance the concept of massive. *The standard disqualifies a butterfly nose (a nose with partial pigment) and a total lack of pigment.*

The Akita's **ears** are unique, unlike those of any other breed. Thick leather ears stand erect, forming into perfect triangles with slightly rounded tips. Smaller in comparison to the head, the wide-spaced ears are carried forward over the eyes in a graceful curve toward the short, powerful neck. When viewed from the side, the 45-degree forward angle of the ears gives an impression of an alert, intelligent dog intently listening for the sound of his owner. When pulled forward, the tip just touches the upper eye rim. *Drop or broken ears are a disqualification.*

The standard gives a concise description of **lips,** noting the Akita has tight, black lips, meaning he does not drool (that is, until he raises his head from a water bowl). The **tongue** is pink but some Akitas have dark spots on their tongues. There is no doubt the Akita has **teeth.** A scissors bite is one in which the upper incisor teeth touch and engage with the lower incisor teeth. This bite promotes a stronger mouth and is preferred in the Akita. A level or even bite causes more wear on the teeth but is accepted. *Disqualifications are a noticeably undershot jaw, where the lower jaw protrudes out further than the upper jaw. The reverse is true in the overshot jaw, another disqualification.*

THE AMERICAN KENNEL CLUB

Familiarly referred to as "the AKC," the American Kennel Club is a nonprofit organization devoted to the advancement of purebred dogs. The AKC maintains a registry of recognized breeds and adopts and enforces rules for dog events including shows, obedience trials, field trials, hunting tests, lure coursing, herding, earthdog trials, agility and the Canine Good Citizen program. It is a club of clubs, established in 1884 and composed, today, of over 500 autonomous dog clubs throughout the United States. Each club is represented by a delegate; the delegates make up the legislative body of the AKC, voting on rules and electing directors. The American Kennel Club maintains the Stud Book, the record of every dog over registered with the AKC, and publishes a variety of materials on purebred dogs, including a monthly magazine, books and numerous educational pamphlets. For more information, contact the AKC at the address listed in Chapter 13, "Resources," and look for the names of their publications in Chapter 12, "Recommended Reading."

Structure and Soundness

The standard mentions a "brisk and powerful" **gait** with "strides of moderate length," a strong, level back and rear legs moving in line with the front legs. Proper structure is a prerequisite to this style gait.

Akitas are typically slightly longer than they are tall.

The standard calls for a short, muscular **neck** widening down to the shoulders, with a pronounced crest or arch blending into the head. The typical Akita **body** is slightly longer than high, with females longer than males. The extra length of the female provides for puppies. A longer body permits sufficient length of stride to prevent the gait from being short and choppy. Measuring from sternum to the buttocks, the standard calls for a 10-to-9 ratio in males and 11-to-9 in females. A male Akita 26 inches tall should be 28.9 inches long; a female of the same height would be 31.8 inches long.

Calling for a wide and deep **chest,** we are to assume the standard writers allow for substantial heart and lung capacity, a goal that requires well-sprung ribs dropped to the elbow and carried well back. A wide, oval-shaped chest will provide width between the front legs, allowing freedom of movement. "Depth of chest is one-half height of dog at shoulder," as stated in the standard, indicates the dog has a good length of leg. These qualities evoke an image of the Akita in a ground-covering run to rescue his owner from harm.

The distance from the bottom of the chest to the floor will be equal to the distance from the top of the shoulder to the bottom of the chest. In other words, if you cut the dog in half horizontally, both pieces would be the same height—but you would no longer have an Akita.

The **back** or topline is always straight and level with a "firmly muscled loin and moderate **tuck-up.**" In translation, it is a waistline of sorts. The tuck-up occurs in front of the loin and when viewed from above, tuck-up gives the appearance of a waistline. *Light bone and rangy body are disqualifying faults.*

The **tail** offsets the imposing head and adds balance to the effect of the dog. When pulled down, the end of the tailbone touches the rear hock. The standard covers this subject in detail. The double curl is acceptable and often preferred by some breeders. *A sickle or uncurled tail is a disqualification.* Some Akitas, when unhappy, hot, tired or bored, may allow their tails to droop. The uncurled tail is not a fault under these conditions.

Forequarters and **hindquarters** are lumped together in the standard.

Akita puppies look like cuddly bear cubs, but they gain nearly 85 pounds in the first year.

In reality, we know the torso separates these anatomical parts. The shoulders are strong and powerful with a moderate layback. Moderate layback means the shoulder blade slopes at an angle of 50 degrees—the upper arm is angled back from the shoulder point and is the same length as the shoulder, setting the leg well under the dog.

The **forelegs** are heavy-boned, thick and straight when viewed from the front. The elbows do not protrude out to the side. The pastern is sloped 15 degrees from vertical when viewed from the side. The pastern is a shock absorber when the dog gaits. The front legs of a correctly moving Akita will incline toward each other while remaining in a vertical line as in a V, but the feet do not touch. *Elbows in or out and loose shoulders are cited as faults.*

The front structure carries through the Akita's image of balance, size and power. The standard's brief description of the **hindquarters** continues the image of strength and stamina. Width and muscular development are comparable to the forequarters, with well-developed upper thighs. The stifle (front of the thigh) should be moderately bent, the hocks straight when viewed from the rear but well let down.

The Akita has a double coat suitable for cold climates and protection from summer heat.

The front **dewclaws,** an obsolete extra toe, are present but the rear dewclaws are usually removed. Akitas have **cat feet,** a description for a round, compact foot, with tightly bunched, well-arched toes with a thick pad. Toes that are flat when the dog stands indicate a weak pastern. Spreading of the toes is called "splayed feet," a term usually denoting a fault. Some large Akita puppies will have splayed feet at four to five months, but grow out of them. When seen from the front, the feet should point straight ahead. Turning east or west is an indication of a weak pastern.

"Gait" is a term used to describe the dog in motion, including walking, pacing, trotting and galloping. It is an important consideration in dog judging since the dog's gait can indicate structural faults not visible to the naked eye, like hip and knee disorders. The standard requires a brisk, purposeful **gait** with strides of moderate length. The back or topline remains level and strong, while the rear legs move in line with the front legs.

Coat Length and Color

As a "Northern breed," the Akita qualifies for a warm, double **coat,** suitable for a cold climate. The woolly undercoat may be a different color than the harsher top coat, which stands out from the body. The double coat acts as insulation against the cold, as well as protection from the heat of summer. Yes, an Akita can live comfortably in a warm climate when you provide lots of shade and fresh water.

The Akita does not shed constantly, but when he does enter his biannual shedding stage, the soft undercoat settles gracefully on the floor in hunks large enough to hide the family cat. This stage will pass quickly; within three months a new coat has replaced the one you collected from the carpet. A few industrious owners save the sheddings to spin into wool.

The standard is very specific on the correct coat length—length of hair at withers and rump approximately two inches. *Any indication of ruff or feathering is considered a fault.* There is a "long-coat" gene in the Akita that produces dogs with lush, long undercoats, well over the acceptable limits mentioned in the standard. Though not welcome in the showring, these lush-coated Akitas are wonderful pets.

Color in the Akita is often a controversial topic, revolving around the definition of a pinto. The standard calls for "any color, including white, brindle or pinto," with clear, brilliant, colors. White Akitas have no mask. Pinto markings are described as a white background with evenly placed patches covering the head and more than one-third of the body. In other words, a pinto should be no more than two-thirds white and one-third another color. The standard does not fault a white Akita with a dark head; the standard writers did not foresee the need to classify these uniquely marked Akitas. The undercoat usually is a different color except on white dogs.

Categorized as the smallest of the giant breeds, the standard writers included height requirements to maintain proper **size.** *Males under 25 inches at the shoulder (wither), females under 23 inches at the shoulder are disqualified from the showring.* The preferred size for a male is 26 to 28 inches and for a female 24 to 26 inches.

The *correct* Akita **temperament** is alert, somewhat aloof with strangers, naturally protective of family and property, very territorial and dominant over other animals. The standard uses the phrase: "aggressive toward other dogs," but the term "aggressive" is often misunderstood. Many breeders wish to see the word replaced with "assertive," or "dominant." Refer to chapter 3 for a more in-depth discussion on the innumerable variations of Akita behavior.

chapter 2

The
Akita's
Ancestry

The Akita is named for her place of origin, the Odate region in Akita Prefecture, on the island of Honshu, in northern Japan. It is an area surrounded on four sides by rugged mountains with cold, snowy winters and wet summers. Magnificent forests filled with Akita cedar trees, vast fields, rolling hills and the Yoneshiro River complement a countryside as beautiful as the Akita herself. Originally, the Akita was called the "Odate dog," but the name was changed to Akitainu when the breed was designated as a Natural Monument in 1931.

The famous Japanese dog Mutci-Go, born in 1956.

15

The Akita's Earliest Ancestors

It is difficult to compile an accurate historical picture of the Akita's ancestry, since few written chronicles pertaining expressly to the origins of the Akita exist. Some archeological discoveries from the Akita region suggest that from 8,000 B.C. to about 200 B.C. the people were hunters, gatherers and fishermen. The dogs that inhabited the area during this time were used as hunting dogs, and called "Matagi-Inu," which translates to "hunting dog." It is likely they were originally brought by Mongoloid invaders from Korea who made contact with the resident seminomadic tribes. There is archeological evidence from these periods indicating that dogs similar in structure and size to today's Akita existed thousands of years ago.

For centuries in Japan, power was held by the Shogun, who dominated and controlled the warrior knights. These warriors gloried in a life of warfare, self-discipline and physical and mental toughening—indifference to suffering was part of this process. Mounted Samurai bowmen teased and killed dogs for sport, but the favorite pastime was dog-fighting. The dog-fights of the twelfth and thirteenth centuries were intensely cruel, with as many as 200 dogs released to fight in a free-for-all.

WHERE DID DOGS COME FROM?

It can be argued that dogs were right there at man's side from the beginning of time. As soon as human beings began to document their own existence, the dog was among their drawings and inscriptions. Dogs were not just friends, they served a purpose: There were dogs to hunt birds, pull sleds, herd sheep, burrow after rats—even sit in laps! What your dog was originally bred to do influences the way it behaves. The American Kennel Club recognizes over 140 breeds, and there are hundreds more distinct breeds around the world. To make sense of the breeds, they are grouped according to their size or function. The AKC has seven groups:

1) Sporting, 2) Working,
3) Herding, 4) Hounds,
5) Terriers, 6) Toys,
7) Non-Sporting

Can you name a breed from each group? Here's some help: (1) Golden Retriever; (2) Doberman Pinscher; (3) Collie; (4) Beagle; (5) Scottish Terrier; (6) Maltese; and (7) Dalmatian. All modern domestic dogs (*Canis familiaris*) are related, however different they look, and are all descended from *Canis lupus*, the gray wolf.

New Age Brings New Dog

The nineteenth century brought industrialization to Japan, along with a need for raw materials. The demand for gold and silver created a mining boom, luring thousands of fortune hunters out of the cities and into the countryside. This influx of humanity into formerly quiet rural areas created a number of social problems, including riots and an increase in crime. For this reason, the Matagi-Inu (hunting dogs) began to be trained as family guardians. Affluent farming families selectively bred their dogs with a special emphasis on size and aggressiveness.

This is Maden Hime-Go, born in 1957. She received the highest Japanese award at the 38th Headquarters Show, the Meiyosho Award.

At the same time, Japan was becoming an attractive island for European traders, who brought their dogs. These animals crossbred with the Matagi-Inu; among them were Mastiffs, Great Danes, Saint Bernards and Bulldogs. Even the powerful Japanese Tosa fighting dog was used in crossbreeding to produce a dog with superior fighting ability. These dogs were called "Shin-Akita" (Improved Dogs).

The Shin-Akita was large, powerful, and distinguished by her coiled tail. Because of the Shin-Akita's popularity, the traditional Japanese dog of the Odate region became a rarity. Fortunately, a few dog fanciers continued to revere the original Japanese breeds, and the quality of the Matagi-Inu was maintained.

The Japanese dog of the late nineteenth century had become a large, athletic, aggressive and courageous dog, but was genetically far removed from the purity of the original Japanese dogs. The Shin-Akita and the Matagi-Inu existed as two separate and distinct types of Japanese Akita. They are the forerunners of the current American Akita and Japanese Akitainu.

Early Breed Restoration

The twentieth century brought a compelling nationalistic movement for the preservation of Japanese objects by some Japanese intellectuals, and the popularity of Western culture began to fade. Landmarks, scenic areas, vegetation and animals were earmarked to be designated as Japanese Natural Monuments, preserving them for the heritage of Japan. In 1919, a law was passed ensuring the existence of these Natural Monuments.

*Luckily for
Akita lovers,
the Japanese
preserved the
breed.*

Impetus from this preservation movement led dog owners in the Odate region to attempt breed restoration. On August 30, 1929, the first Akita dog registry, listing thirty dogs, was published. Strict regulations and application procedures were set up to assure the preservation of the Akita and forbid further crossbreeding.

Establishment of the Akita-Inu

Japanese dog fanciers purchased the rare and comparatively pure Japanese dogs living in the rural Matagi villages to use in the restoration process. In July 1931, the Odate dog was designated a Japanese Natural Monument, and the name Akita-Inu was used for the first time.

Hachi-Ko, a Living Legend

On October 4, 1932, newspapers published an article entitled "A Touching Aging Dog's Story, A Seven Year Wait For His Master's Return." This was the story of Hachi-Ko. Hachi-Ko was born in November 1923 in Akita Prefecture. The puppy grew up to become the most famous Akita in Japanese history. Professor Eizaburo Ueno, who taught at Tokyo Imperial University, was a great animal lover and had always dreamed of owning an Akita dog.

The professor's dreams became reality when one of his students, working in the government offices of Akita Prefecture, sent him an Akita puppy. The professor named the cream-colored puppy Hachi, but called him Hachi-Ko ("Ko" being a Japanese term of endearment). In typical Akita fashion, Hachi-Ko soon bonded for life with the aging professor.

Each morning, accompanied by Hachi-Ko, the professor walked a short distance from his home to the Shibuya train station and boarded the train. Hachi-Ko stayed behind waiting for the professor's daily return. One spring afternoon in 1925, Hachi-Ko waited, as always, for the return of his master. But on this day there was no rendezvous— Professor Ueno had died of a stroke at the university. With stoic Akita loyalty, Hachi-Ko stood vigil long into the night, and had friends of the professor's not taken him in to shelter, he would undoubtedly have waited a lifetime.

Hachi-Ko was sent several miles away to live with relatives of the deceased professor; but he persistently ran back to the home where he had once lived with his beloved professor. From his former home, Hachi-Ko went directly to the Shibuya station to take up his vigil. The dog waited in vain for the return of the person to whom he had devoted his life. Kikuzaboro Kobayashi, Professor Ueno's former gardener, who had always

FAMOUS OWNERS OF AKITAS

Helen Keller

Shari Lewis

Linda Ronstadt

Dudley Moore

Cher

Cal Ripken Jr.

Dan Akroyd

Whitney Houston

Sugar Ray Robinson

liked Hachi-Ko, fed and watched over the Akita, and allowed him to mourn and wait for his master. When Chuichi Yoshikawa became the director of the Shibuya station, he took an instant liking to Hachi-Ko and cared for him.

During Hachi-Ko's twelve years, the loyalty and devotion shown his master turned the Akita into a living legend and a national hero. A bronze statue of Hachi-Ko was built at the Shibuya station. During this revival of Japanese traditionalism, the statue and the Akita's story served as an example of loyalty to children in Japanese primary schools.

It is written that when Hachi-Ko died on March 8, 1935, a national day of mourning was declared throughout the country. His statue was covered with flowers, and the burning of incense sent clouds of smoke over the area. This great Akita is remembered in Japan every March. The original statue of Hachi-Ko was destroyed during World War II when the bronze was melted down and used for weapons production. But a new statue was built at the Shibuya station site in 1948, and it stands today as a testament to the loyalty, trust and intelligence of the Akita dog.

Helen Keller (left) with her Akita, Kenzan-Go, and her companion, Polly Thomson, taken in 1939.

Helen Keller's Akita

Helen Keller was the first celebrated American to own an Akita. Her affection for the breed created considerable interest in the press and among dog fanciers.

During a visit to Japan in 1937, Helen Keller was told the story of Hachi-Ko and thereafter asked her Japanese hosts to introduce her to the breed. It was here that she met Kamikaze-Go, a two-month-old Akita puppy who was to become the first Akita to enter the United States. "Kami" went to live with Miss Keller at her Long Island estate but, sadly, died from distemper at the age of seven months.

Helen Keller sent to Japan for another Akita, but a growing climate of Japanese-American political tensions delayed her requests for a new Akita until 1939, when Kenzan-Go, Kami's litter-brother, was sent to Miss Keller. Kenzan-Go lived to be about seven or eight years old.

Helen Keller's personal writings were filled with her love of Kami and Kenzan-Go, whom she affectionately called "Go-Go." Of Kami, she wrote: "If ever there was an angel in fur it was Kamikaze. I know I shall never feel quite the same tenderness for any other pet. The Akita dog has all the qualities that appeal to me—he is gentle, companionable and trusty—I never saw such devotion in a five-months-old puppy."

Akitas have grown increasingly popular in the United States since servicemen brought them to this country after World War II.

"The O.J. Dog"

In 1995, the murder of Nicole Brown Simpson and her friend, Ronald Goldman, brought unwarranted attention to Kato, the family Akita. No one will ever know what happened that night, if the Akita was the only witness to a double murder or simply the first to arrive at the scene. The tabloids labeled Kato a "hero" for leading neighbors back to the crime scene, opening the door to exploitation of the breed.

Akitas were called "the O.J. dog," and the notoriety brought with it an increased popularity—everyone wanted their own "Kato." The Akita was returned to the Brown family, where he lives with Nicole's surviving children. But Kato was not the only Akita owned by a

*The Akita's
nobility is what
has endeared
him to people
for centuries.*

well-known personality. Helen Keller, Shari Lewis, Jobeth Williams, Ricky Watters, Tyne Daly, Linda Ronstadt, Dudley Moore, Cher, Susan Anton, Pia Zadora, Cal Ripken Jr., Pat Harrington, Dan Akroyd, Yoko Ono, Elvis Stojiko, Tree Rollins, Whitney Houston, Christian Slater, Mitch Williams, Cheech Marin, Sugar Ray Robinson, Kerry King and Susan Cabot are all Akita fanciers.

An Increasingly Popular Dog

The popularity of Akitas continues to grow as the breed captivates novices. The United States has the largest population of Akitas outside Japan, especially on the West Coast. The Canadian Kennel Club recognized Akitas in 1975. The Akita Club of Canada, the Akita Club of British Columbia and the Akita Club of Alberta continue to promote the breed, which is expected to grow in popularity, particularly because the Akita is naturally tolerant of extremes of weather and is admirably suited to the diversity of the Canadian landscape. The numbers of Akita fanciers in Mexico, England, Germany, Holland, New Zealand, Australia, Sweden, Norway and Finland have also grown steadily.

chapter 3

The World
According to the
Akita

Owning a dog is a responsibility that includes a great deal more than just feeding the animal. This is especially true of the Akita—each Akita comes into the world believing he is the pack leader.

Dogs are pack animals and follow a complex hierarchy centering around the pack leader, or the "alpha" member. The purpose of the pack is survival; therefore, the pack leader is respected by the pack for his intelligence, ability to lead the

hunt and to provide protection. The alpha dog is not vicious or aggressive, he is a strong, assertive leader. To reinforce his position, the alpha dog dominates the pack using eye contact, growls and body language.

It is important that you establish yourself as the pack leader through consistent control over your Akita from the first days you bring him home. This control begins immediately with a task as simple as housebreaking and continues through all the varied training stages. Once the hierarchy is clearly established, your Akita will look to you for guidance before making his own decisions because you are the most respected member of the pack.

Akitas are natural guard dogs, and getting them out and about while being a firm leader is key to their social ability.

Akitas Are Pack Leaders

You can recognize that you have a pack leader dog by his "take-charge" attitude; a need to control, to lead the pack. In Akitas, this behavior is displayed in males more often than in bitches and usually begins between the age of nine months to two years.

A challenge to authority can be as innocent as ignoring a command or as blatant as a growl. If you allow a growl to go unchallenged, you send a clear signal to the dog that he need not respect your authority. The results of such a decision may be very serious. Your ultimate goal in working with an alpha dog is mutual respect, which can be accomplished without destroying the wonderful spirit of an Akita.

Socialization Is Key

You cannot simply leave your Akita in your backyard and ignore him. Socialization of your Akita puppy is essential to turning him into a well-rounded, confident companion (see chapter 4). Akitas thrive on human companionship and should be household members, not simply yard dogs. If you purchased an Akita hoping to have a guard dog, allow him the full responsibility of guarding you and his entire property. Your house, especially the front door and windows, are accessible to a determined intruder, and if your Akita lives in the backyard, he cannot protect your property effectively.

The breed standard allows Akita aggression "toward other dogs." To be sure, Akitas are protective and territorial. Any male Akita allowed to roam the neighborhood will eventually include the entire neighborhood as his territory. He will begin marking boundaries that range as far as he does. Any animal within those boundaries will be subjected to your Akita's dominance. If the Akita is not arguing boundaries with other dogs, he might be out hunting the neighbors' cats. For those and other reasons, nuisance dog legislation enacted in many cities and municipalities forbids free-roaming dogs. Confinement in a fenced yard or a secure kennel is the clear solution.

Intelligent, Independent

Inside that huge bearlike head is an extremely intelligent mind. The Akita has an innate ability to think for himself and a very independent nature, often confused for stubbornness or a lack of trainability. More often, however, it is simply the case that an Akita learns quickly and gets bored easily.

INSTINCTIVE GUARDIAN

Akitas are intelligent and discerning, two important characteristics for a good guard dog. Although not habitual barkers, an Akita's sensitivity to unfamiliar sounds or strange dogs or people appearing in their domain, will usually result in aggressive barking.

Generally, when you invite guests into your home, your Akita will sense your receptive attitude and welcome them as well. However, strangers are not welcome in the home of an Akita whose owners are absent, and the ever-discerning Akita can recognize the difference between a guest and a prowler. Kuma, a large male, was placed by Akita Rescue Society of America (ARSA) with a loving family in Oregon. Kuma had been with them less than three months when an intruder made the luckless decision to burglarize the family's property when they were absent. The burglar later told police that when he jumped the back fence, Kuma chased him under the motor home. "He could have crawled in after me," he reported, "but he just kept circling and every time I tried to roll out the other side he was waiting for me, snapping at my legs." The ordeal went on for over two hours until the mailman heard the burglar's cries for help.

Because Akitas are protective and territorial, they should be kept in a securely fenced yard when not on leash or inside with their owners.

Again, this demonstrates the Akita's ability to think through a situation and act with restraint. Kuma knew that his family was away, but he also knew they did not give permission for anyone to climb over the fence and remove property.

The stories of Akitas successfully guarding their owners or their owners' property are too many to enumerate. It is precisely because of their strength, courage, intimidating demeanor and reputation as exemplary guard dogs that Akitas help their owners to feel fully secure.

Akitas and Children

Akitas and children can develop a wonderful relationship, but the success or failure of this potential relationship depends on you, the behavior of the children, and the temperament of the Akita. Akita puppies raised with children are usually good with them. Problems can arise when the dog is older and protective of "its children" when their playmates are unsupervised in the dog's environment. The play of toddlers can be free-spirited, noisy and very active. Screaming, running, wrestling and other hands-on play between your children and their friends can invoke an Akita's protective instincts and be interpreted as aggression toward his child, and the Akita may respond with aggression.

Akitas are great with children under the right circumstances.

Some children treat animals with respect and kindness, while other children are abusive and inconsiderate. An Akita will not always tolerate abuse from a child, especially if that child does not belong to the Akita. It is important at all times to supervise children at play when an Akita is present. If you do not have children in your home, take your puppy over to school playgrounds. Ask the neighborhood children to come visit your puppy a few times weekly. You must get him used to children to the extent that he understands and respects their smaller size. Even the largest of Akitas can be taught to move carefully around small children.

Socializing the Akita puppy to respect children is especially important if you plan to have children during the lifetime of your dog.

If you have many children in your home and an open-door policy for neighborhood children, then an Akita is probably not the right dog for you. The constant commotion and activity of groups of children is not a compatible mix with a guard dog like an Akita.

Akitas and Other Animals

With Dogs   As a rule, a male and a female Akita will live together in harmony. When two Akitas of the opposite sex live together, the male is usually tolerant of the bitch, often allowing her to dominate. Occasionally he demands total submission; especially when she carries her bullying too far, or when food is present. Most male Akitas already established in a household will readily welcome the addition of a female companion and playmate.

In contrast, a resident female is more likely to be bossy and less tolerant to the introduction of a male into her territory, at least for the first few weeks. She may set up "relationship rules" on her terms. She may even instigate a quarrel or two, but most females eventually accept a male.

Keeping two adult male Akitas together in the same home is rarely successful. Raising two males together as puppies is not usually a problem, but with the onset of sexual development (nine months to one year of age), they are prone to fight, and may cause serious injury to one another. Two female Akitas can be raised together peacefully until one comes into heat and then, in nearly every case, a fight is the probable outcome. Once two Akitas fight, it is difficult to reestablish a peaceful coexistence.

It is easier to keep an Akita with a dog of a different breed and the same sex successfully, especially when there is a disparity in size and temperament. Under such circumstances, the Akita naturally assumes the dominant role. The attitude of the owner is essential to the success of mixing dogs in a home because Akitas are sensitive to the feelings of their owner. If you are convinced your Akita will attack another animal, he probably will oblige. If you are relaxed and confident of your ability to handle and control your dogs, chances are they will feel relaxed and confident in each other's company.

With Cats Many people who enjoy cats seem to be attracted to the catlike qualities of the Akita. An Akita cleans his face after eating, grooms himself and stalks silently and low to the ground when hunting. This does not mean Akitas are perfect companions for cats. A lot depends upon which animal was first in the home. An Akita puppy will usually fit into a home with cats and enjoy their company. In fact, an adult cat will often train a puppy to understand her rules. The Akita will soon outgrow the cat, but can continue to respect and consider her a family member if that relationship was established early.

Angel was a young female Akita whose short life was filled with abuse and neglect until she was rescued by the Akita Rescue Society of America. She was adopted into a family with two white Persian kittens. Both kittens had already established their careers as "actors" in television commercials. From the moment of her arrival, the cats rejected Angel, ignoring all attempts to make friends.

One day Angel discovered a long piece of ribbon near the trash.

A DOG'S SENSES

Sight: With their eyes located farther apart than ours, dogs can detect movement at a greater distance than we can, but they can't see as well up close. They can also see better in less light, but can't distinguish many colors.

Sound: Dogs can hear about four times better than we can, and they can hear high-pitched sounds especially well. Their ancestors, the wolves, howled to let other wolves know where they were; our dogs do the same, but they have a wider range of vocalizations, including barks, whimpers, moans and whines.

Smell: A dog's nose is his greatest sensory organ. His sense of smell is so great he can follow a trail that's weeks old, detect odors diluted to one-millionth the concentration we'd need to notice them, even sniff out a person under water!

Taste: Dogs have fewer taste buds than we do, so they're likelier to try anything—and usually do, which is why it's especially important for their owners to monitor their food intake. Dogs are omnivores, which means they eat meat as well as vegetable matter like grasses and weeds.

Touch: Dogs are social animals and love to be petted, groomed and played with.

*Akitas are
adaptable to
just about any
outdoor activity,
and will gladly
accompany you
on hikes (don't
forget water!).*

Taking one end into her mouth, Angel moved back and forth near the cats, trailing the ribbon in an obvious attempt to invite play. What cat could ever resist a trailing ribbon? Both cats took after the ribbon and the three animals have been friends ever since.

With Livestock   Many Akitas live on ranches with livestock, including goats and sheep. If raised with these animals, most Akitas will accept and protect them. Horses, cows and other large animals are also compatible with Akitas. Yet, even the most docile Akita will not regard chickens and ducks as family members, but will more likely look on them as food.

Before you select an Akita for a family farm or ranch, keep in mind they are not a herding breed; they are a working breed, more ideally suited to hunting and guarding. Therefore, obedience training is important before allowing an Akita to roam freely with baby lambs, goats and other smaller farm animals.

Outdoor Activities

This truly unique breed has physical characteristics that make him adaptable for just about any outdoor activity. It is a double-coated breed that thrives in cold climates. He is soft-mouthed and silent, with keen eyes and a sensitive nose, an instinctive hunter and a natural tracker. The Akita has webbed feet and can swim with grace and power.

Sledding   For the outdoor enthusiast with a structurally sound Akita, the sport of sledding might be of interest. Anyone who has ever walked an Akita on a leash knows he has an instinctive desire to pull. This ability, along with his great strength and size, makes the Akita a good candidate for sledding. Before starting your Akita in this sport, you must educate yourself about proper training techniques and the correct use of harnesses to prevent injury to your dog. In addition, there are specific rules governing the sport, which have been formulated by sledding organizations. If you are not interested in becoming involved in the competitive aspects of the sport you might consider having fun with your Akita in a noncompetitive setting. Building a cart for a child and training your Akita to pull in harness can provide hours of enjoyment.

CHARACTERISTICS OF THE AKITA
Loyal
Dignified
Affectionate
Intelligent
Stubborn
Protective
Dominant

Hiking and Camping If you are enthusiastic about outdoor sports like hiking, camping and backpacking, you already have something in common with all Akitas. The moderate angulation of the Akita makes him suitable for climbing hills and even rugged mountainous terrain. To begin any of these activities with your Akita, you must take him through basic obedience training to guarantee he will stay by your side or within view. Once this is accomplished, begin his outdoor training by having him wear empty packs. Even though an Akita can carry approximately 30 percent of his own weight over a great distance, you should introduce weight into the packs gradually. Your enjoyment of the great outdoors will be enhanced when you experience the world through the eyes and nose of an Akita. (See chapter 9 for other activities to share with your Akita.)

Delightful Companions

Life with an Akita is rarely boring. It is filled with affection, fun and surprises. Devotion to his pack combined with a creative streak gave Kaleb's family a memorable story to share with friends. Eighteen-month-old Kaleb was placed with a young couple after adoption from an animal shelter. Phil and Debbie rewarded the Akita's impeccable house manners by granting Kaleb house privileges while they went out to dinner.

Bored? Lonely? Perhaps a little of each, Kaleb entered the bedroom, turned the knob to open the closet, then neatly removed articles of clothing to carry into the living room. Kaleb carefully built a pile of clothing for each person. Shoes were followed by a skirt and blouse belonging to Debbie, cautiously arranged next to Phil's shoes, pants and a shirt. Satisfied with the creation, Kaleb fell asleep touching both sets of clothing.

Phil and Debbie returned to find Kaleb's fashion show. They were amazed how carefully the big Akita had deposited their clothes. Of course, Kaleb was not disciplined—they were flattered by a dog who loved them enough to re-create their images for company when he was alone.

While You're Away

An Akita less creative than Kaleb can be content in a household where the family is absent at work or school if time is set aside each day for quality time between dog and owner. Similarly, Akitas adapt well to apartment living, provided their owners make time for a few daily exercise periods. With proper attention and training, an Akita will respond with unlimited versatility to almost any lifestyle.

To become a full-fledged household member is the ideal situation for an Akita. In this case, he will want to spend most of his time in the house with you, but as a puppy, he will not understand the correlation between this privilege and good behavior.

Bad Habits

Usually, destructive behavior like chewing furniture, digging up trees or destroying the patio furniture occurs when a dog is bored or lonely. You can easily correct furniture chewing if you are present when the dog is loose in the home, but when you are not home, your Akita should not be given free range of the home until he is a mature dog. Until you are confident that your Akita has been trained to think through temptation, leave him crated, kenneled or in his yard with enough toys to prevent boredom. A floss toss or two, some rawhide chews or a soccer ball are all perfect entertainment.

If your Akita appears to have boundless energy during these hours alone in the yard, you might arrange your schedule to provide for a long walk before you leave him alone. A tired Akita will usually sleep and build up energy for your return, and energy expended in supervised exercise will not be used in digging or chewing.

Mature or adult Akitas who have access to the home through a doggy door rarely abuse this privilege, practicing instead the good manners they have been taught by respecting your belongings. Destructive dogs are always those who seek attention from their owners. Examine your lifestyle closely. Are you spending enough quality time with your Akita? Does the dog get enough exercise? Dogs that are simply left in their yards do not exercise themselves: They need structured exercise and active play periods. Set aside the time needed to satisfy your dog's craving for attention.

Akitas are devoted companions, as the author's dog demonstrates.

Digging is another destructive yet natural instinct of dogs, including Akitas. The best way to handle digging is to provide an area for your dog where he is allowed to dig as deep as he pleases. I have selected a spot under a pineapple-guava bush. The spot was selected first by my dogs and then encouraged by me because it is an area away from any walkways and unseen by guests. My dogs have continued to use the same dig hole for years without starting a hole in the middle of the lawn.

When your dog digs a hole in a permissible area, praise him and then bring the dog to the spot you have selected. Soften the earth for him, begin digging a bit and encourage him to continue.

The Akita is big and powerful, intelligent yet stubborn, aggressive but protective; he is also beautiful and dignified, gentle and extremely sensitive. An Akita loves to carry objects in his mouth: an envelope, the newspaper, a toy, your shoe, even the Sunday newspapers. He will take your wrist gently between his powerful jaws then lead you to the cookie cupboard or to his leash. The Akita greets you after an absence bearing gifts—a ball, an old chew, a twig, your glasses. You respond by offering your open hand to receive the offering, which is a demonstration of their happiness to have you home.

Your Akita will rapidly dance a four-step in a perfect circle, wooo-wooo-woooing to proclaim his happiness. The Akita "Happy Fit" is another demonstration of sheer delight. Suddenly the Akita charges through the house, jumps onto a bed, circles long enough to remove the bedding, orbits around you, then begins another round. A waving paw asks for attention, a playbow invites a game or two. He will talk, murmur and wooo a complaint or comment, and heave a heavy sigh of contentment as he settles down to rest.

MORE INFORMATION ON AKITAS

NATIONAL BREED CLUB

Akita Club of America, Inc.
Janet Voss
1016 Vermont Road
Woodstock, IL 60098
(815) 338-9293

The club sends information on breed history and characteristics.

HEALTH INFORMATION PACKAGE

Delaware Valley Akita Rescue
P.O. Box 578
Rancocas, NJ 08073
(609) 859-3125

DVAR offers a comprehensive, up-to-date information package on health problems.

BOOKS

Bouyet, Barbara. *Akita-Treasure of Japan*. Strafford, Pa.: International Marketing, 1992.

Brearley, Joan McDonald. *The Book of the Akita*. Neptune, N.J.: TFH Publications, 1985.

Linderman, Joan, and Virginia Funk. *The New Complete Akita*. New York: Howell Book House, 1994.

Van Der Lyn, Edita. *Akitas*. Neptune, N.J.: TFH Publications, 1988.

MAGAZINES

Akita World
Hoflin Publishing, Inc.
4401 Zephyr Street
Wheat Ridge, CO 80033-3209

VIDEOS

American Kennel Club, *Akitas*.

Living

with an

part two

Akita

Bringing Your
Akita
Home

Akitas are gaining in popularity. They are often seen in television commercials and magazine advertisements. They were labeled the "Yuppie dog of the Eighties," and are often photographed with celebrity owners. But popularity has drawbacks—it invites irresponsible breeding by people interested only in money. As a result, acquiring a quality puppy may require some effort and careful consideration.

The Right Akita For You

In choosing a pet Akita, if you have small children, you will not want an alpha Akita (one that continually seeks to dominate her pack). Alpha dogs require more time, attention, training, socialization and control than more submissive Akitas. With children in your home, you may not have the time to turn an alpha dog into an acceptable children's pet. You would be better off with a calm, submissive Akita, one with a gentle nature, willing to please.

The temperament of the puppy is very important. Personality traits are not an accident of nature, but a genetic certainty. Ask about your puppy's parents and try to meet them before you get your pup. If one or both parents are too aggressive to approach, you are probably going to have a puppy with a similar temperament.

Your puppy should be responsive and confident but not a bully.

Carefully look at the parents for health problems. Do they have skin and coat problems, hot spots, sores, dry, flaky skin, or bald patches? Are their eyes running? Do they look healthy and well cared for? Are they alert and active? Health problems tend to be inherited, and thus any problems in the parents may foretell difficulties you will encounter with your puppy.

What to Look For

Look for a puppy who enjoys her littermates but will seek to make friends with you. She should be curious and slightly bold, as well as friendly and confident. She should tolerate handling and be responsive to affection. Avoid the aggressive bully who is relentless in pursuit of something, and the withdrawn, timid little pup, no matter how cute and pathetic she is.

Sex is a factor in temperament. Usually females have a gentler nature, and their smaller size makes them easier to control. Females also tend to be more tolerant of children than males. The males, being much larger, can be harder to control. Male aggression toward other males is important to consider. However, male/female differences are generalities, since some females are more aggressive and dominant than some males.

Puppy's Basic Supplies

Before your puppy comes home, go on a shopping spree at your local pet supply store. After you load the cart with whatever food you selected, add stainless steel food and water bowls. (Plastic may be cheaper but it has been linked to outbreaks of "puppy acne.") You will need a two-foot-square, nonslide rubber mat to go under the water bowl to catch spillage. Whenever an Akita drinks water, there is "spillage." A large shallow pan or foil oven liner will serve as a catch basin.

**PUPPY
ESSENTIALS**

Your new
puppy will
need:

food bowl

water bowl

collar

leash

I.D. tag

bed

crate

toys

grooming
supplies

Since chewing is a normal canine instinct, you need something permissible to chew in place of your fingers, the furniture or your clothing. Small rawhide chews, flavored chew toys, and hard rubber toys are suitable for an Akita puppy. Hickory-smoked, sterilized bones can be filled with peanut butter or a favorite treat to provide hours of entertainment. Include a wire brush and steel comb to begin grooming and an adjustable nylon collar and leash.

Wait! There's more. A long-handled poop-scoop will come in handy, especially as the puppy grows. A small trash can with a tight lid and appropriate-size plastic bags makes a good potty-can to contain body waste until you can dispose of it.

Clean-up is one of the first rules of housebreaking. A puppy's natural tendency is to return to the place where she has gone before. Removing the stain and odor will discourage the puppy from returning to that prized Persian carpet in the entryway. You need a good chemical carpet cleaner/deodorizer; there are many available. Toss in a carpet brush, add a few baby gates to prevent the puppy from roaming the house unattended and you are ready to bring the baby home.

Puppy Comes Home

When first bringing the puppy home, allow her time to become accustomed to her new home and family. It is important she becomes socialized in her home before taking her out into the streets.

This is also an ideal time to introduce her to her first collar and lead. Do this by putting the collar on first. Your puppy may spin in circles, or roll on the floor or ground in an attempt to rid herself of the collar. She may even bark or whine out of annoyance, and for many days to follow, she will stop spontaneously and scratch at the collar.

Your puppy will need a sturdy leash and a collar. This is a lightweight show collar.

Once the puppy is comfortable with this strange new thing around her neck, attach the leash and call her to you. Do this for short periods each day, but *never* leave her alone with the leash attached.

If you are planning a show career for your Akita, now is the time to begin training her to stand in place. Get her used to the type of handling she will face in a showring.

Game-playing further strengthens the bond between you and your puppy. Playing fetch (throwing a small object for a short distance) will encourage her to retrieve. Lying on the ground and letting the puppy pounce on you much the same way she would play with a littermate helps further the bonding. Hide-and-seek, chase and catch me, splashing games with a water bowl or barking on all fours are all healthy games to play with your

41

puppy. Think dog and you'll come up with some good ideas for puppy play.

If your puppy's play gets too rough, use your hand to slow her down and begin to teach the voice command, "gently." Too much roughhousing teaches the puppy to be rough, and this type of play can carry over into adulthood. When a large dog plays roughly, she can easily cause injury. Do not play fierce tug-of-war games with your Akita; this type of combative play can damage her teeth and escalate into a serious battle for pack leadership.

HOUSEHOLD DANGERS

Curious puppies and inquisitive dogs get into trouble not because they are bad, but simply because they want to investigate the world around them. It's our job to protect our dogs from harmful substances, like the following:

IN THE HOUSE

cleaners, especially pine oil

perfumes, colognes, aftershaves

medications, vitamins

office and craft supplies

electric cords

chicken or turkey bones

chocolate

some house and garden plants, like ivy, oleander and poinsettia

IN THE GARAGE

antifreeze

garden supplies, like snail and slug bait, pesticides, fertilizers, mouse and rat poisons

Socializing Your Pup

Socialization is the vital first step in molding your Akita into a valuable companion dog. Ideally, trips for socialization should occur at least four times a week. When she is four to six months old, her socialization should expand to include an obedience class with you. This is where she will receive additional training in the presence of other dogs. From thirteen weeks on, your puppy is ready to be taken out into the wide world. One note of caution—make sure your puppy has been receiving her vaccinations before you allow her to put one paw out the front door.

When you are ready to venture out, begin by taking her to shopping centers and malls on her leash. Many people will stop to ask about your puppy and to pet her. Take your puppy on walks through parking lots during heavy traffic hours. Take her for a stroll down a busy boulevard. Allow her to familiarize herself with ordinary objects that you take for granted, like a fire hydrant, a lamppost, a mailbox and bicycles.

Let her hear the noise, see the world and meet people, and your Akita will mature into a confident, fearless companion.

A reminder: most cities and towns have strict laws governing clean-up of pet waste, and there are many convenient portable "poop-scoops" available for the pet owner. To be sure your puppy is welcomed back after her initial socialization outings, be diligent in cleaning up after it.

Socialization inside the puppy's "den," your home, is important if you plan to have houseguests in the future. She will learn to distinguish between an invited guest and an uninvited one. She must learn to accept people into her home when you allow them to enter. If you put the puppy outside when you have guests, you are teaching her to resent visitors and, in time, she will be aggressive toward all your guests. Integrate the puppy into your household—she is the newest family member.

After thirteen weeks, your puppy is ready to meet the world. Take her everywhere you can with you.

Common-Sense Training

During the thirteenth through sixteenth weeks it may be necessary to impose some controls on your puppy's emerging personality. Her position within the pack (or your home) is now being established and she may challenge authority as a way of helping her determine her place in the hierarchy. *It is vitally important you never allow an adolescent puppy to get away with defiant behavior.* At all times, she must respect not only your wishes and demands but also those of every human in your family. A large adult Akita who is spoiled and willful may become a dangerous liability.

You may have to meet some challenges with minor discipline at this stage. This is, therefore, a good time to begin teaching your puppy some basic obedience lessons such as: sit; come; controlled walking on a lead. You need not be concerned that consistent obedience training will dampen your Akita's spirit.

Puppies are like children—they require love, affection, time and nurturing. They also require rules, regulations, patience, consistency and discipline when necessary. You can best gain the respect of your Akita through use of eye contact, body language and voice.

HER NAME, AND "NO"

Teach your puppy some basic obedience, like "sit," to help her mind her manners.

You should begin the training process by teaching two words: "No" and her name. At first you may have some difficulty reminding yourself that your puppy will understand only one or two simple words. If you throw an entire barrage of words at your puppy such as: "No, Sumo, don't piddle on the rug, it ruins the expensive carpet," she won't understand. She may understand her name, but the rest will be meaningless. Instead, begin with simple, single-word commands.

Crate Training

Next to housebreaking, crate training your Akita is probably the highest priority in training, and many potential problems can be avoided if you begin crate training your puppy at the earliest opportunity. It is best to invest in an adult-size wire crate that will allow enough room for a grown dog to stretch out comfortably. Initially, the crate will be too large for the puppy, but you can use the extra space for a water bowl (water troughs or cups are available that hook onto the inside wall or door of the crate), toys and a blanket. Akitas grow so quickly that the puppy will soon fit the crate. Training your Akita puppy to spend time in her crate should begin from the first day you bring her home. Although this may at first appear to be somewhat harsh, think about a crate as the dog's den or bedroom—a sanctuary. Dogs are den animals, and to them a crate is a perfectly acceptable pseudo-den and not a prison or cage. Never use the crate as punishment but as an extension of the dog's normal environment. (For more on crate training, see Chapter 8.)

Your Akita will learn all sorts of things in obedience classes. This dog does the "recall" (come) in competition.

Traveling with Your Akita

The crate is very useful if you are taking your Akita traveling. In an automobile, your dog has a greater degree of safety if riding inside her crate. You can leave the car windows down without fear she will leave a moving vehicle. In an accident, a crate will protect your dog the way your seat belt protects you.

On overnight or extended trips, staying in motels is much easier when your dog is crate trained.

Housetraining

A crate-trained puppy will be much easier to housebreak because she will have a distinct dislike of soiling her living space. After feeding and watering your puppy, take her for her walk or put her out into her yard until she has relieved herself.

When she has finished urinating and/or defecating, you can allow her some free house time without fear that she will soil the carpet. After a supervised period of play, take your puppy out again before crating her. To emphasize the housebreaking lesson, each time you take your puppy from her crate to relieve herself, you may wish to do so on a leash to prevent her dashing into another room to relieve herself. (Housetraining is explained fully in Chapter 8.)

Akita Particulars

As already mentioned, Akitas are natural leaders, and take being alpha (Number One) seriously. To discipline an Akita for an alpha challenge, you must be able to figure out when a challenge has occurred. Because eye contact is used by an Akita to convey a challenge or to intimidate, eye contact can also be an effective tool of discipline. Make eye contact with your Akita and hold that eye contact until the dog looks away. When it breaks the contact, offer assurances: "Okay, good girl."

A responsive Akita does not show aggression toward her owner, but instead always tempers her instinctive alpha behavior with the good sense you have taught her. Often eye contact is used by a confident dog who is simply seeking direction—she will look you straight in the eye and ask: "What's next, boss?" When you spend quality time with your Akita you will soon learn what her body language means.

Intentionally ignoring a known command is another way an Akita can challenge. I call it "sudden deaf syndrome!" Go back to step one in the basic training of that command and follow through.

Obedience School

With an Akita, I recommend that you enroll in obedience classes even if you teach your dog basic manners. Classes are the perfect place to teach your Akita that animal aggression is totally unacceptable. With the help of an obedience instructor, you can set up situations to correct aggressive acts toward other dogs, which should be brought to stand just a few inches away from your Akita. In a controlled environment you can be prepared, ready to correct any aggressive behavior. Home training will teach her the basics of Sit, Stay, Down, Come and Heel, but it will not correct aggression toward other dogs.

Finding an obedience school is not difficult. The easiest way is by referral from other Akita owners (see Chapter 13 for resources). If this fails, begin your own investigation. Most parks and recreation departments conduct dog obedience classes. Attend one to meet the instructor and see if you and your dog are comfortable with that person and whether or not the instructor is familiar with Akitas.

Once you have been working with your dog for several months and she has graduated from a formal obedience class, you can assume she will understand that disobedience receives correction. I do not like the word punishment as it applies to animals. The word punish is frequently defined as "rough or injurious treatment," something a dog should never experience. If you lose control of yourself, failure rests with you, not you dog. A better alternative to punishment is reinforcement of learned behavior and follow-through with calm correction. The best training strategies use rewards, which can be either verbal or edible, but in all cases, immediate. Use any wonderful words you choose; your Akita won't know what they mean but she will understand the happiness in your voice.

JAPANESE NAMES FOR YOUR AKITA (AND THEIR TRANSLATIONS)	
Kitsune	Fox
Kinu	Silk
Sakura	Cherry
Ringo	Apple
Hoshi	Star
Hana	Blossom
Tomodachi	Friend
Kuroi	Black
Shogun	A leader
Kashi	Oak
Sato	Sugar
Natsu	Summer
Samurai	Warrior
Shiro	White
Riko	Clever
Shinju	Pearl

chapter 5

Feeding
Your
Akita

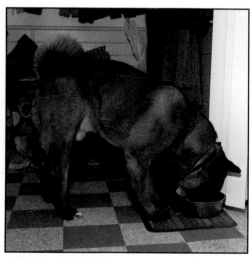

A proper diet is essential to your Akita's healthy growth. In Japan, Akitas thrived on rice, seaweed and some fish, but now they must adapt to commercial dog foods. With well over 150 types of dry dog food, and 50 or more brands of canned dog food to choose from, selecting the healthiest diet for your Akita can be a perplexing chore.

With some basic knowledge of the components of a healthy, balanced dog food, and an awareness of the special dietary needs of the Akita, you should have no problem picking the right combination of foods for your dog. "Canned or dry food?" Dry! Canned food as a dietary staple would be cost-prohibitive since each can of food contains 75 percent moisture. You would need at least eight to ten cans a day to feed an adult Akita.

Basic Nutrition

You should become an avid label reader, because most of the popularly advertised foods available in supermarkets are totally inadequate to meet the nutritional requirements of an Akita. Often, these commercial foods include soybean products as one of the main sources of protein. This plant protein is unsatisfactory for an Akita because soybean products lack some essential amino acids necessary to build protein. Essential amino acids are those not produced in the body.

The majority of protein in the food you select must be from animal sources such as chicken, turkey, fish, and meat. An Akita will do well on a meat-based food with rice or wheat. The protein content should be between 22 and 26 percent, and the fat content 7 to 18 percent. Older dogs should receive less protein and fat in their diet. Dog foods that meet these criteria for protein and fat content are called "premium" foods.

While searching for an all-natural or near-natural quality dry dog food, keep in mind that high-quality protein is easily digested and assimilated. This includes protein found in chicken, turkey, beef, fish and dairy products such as eggs, cheese and milk, as well as small amounts of lamb. You can, of course, cook for your dog, but it

---

TYPES OF FOODS/TREATS

There are three types of commercially available dog food—dry, canned and semimoist—and a huge assortment of treats (lucky dogs!) to feed your dog. Which should you choose?

Dry and canned foods contain similar ingredients. The primary difference between them is their moisture content. The moisture is not just water. It's blood and broth, too, the very things that dogs adore. So while canned food is more palatable, dry food is more economical, convenient and effective in controlling tartar buildup. Most owners feed a 25% canned/75% dry diet to give their dogs the benefit of both. Just be sure your dog is getting the nutrition he needs (you and your veterinarian can determine this).

Semimoist foods have the flavor dogs love and the convenience owners want. However, they tend to contain excessive amounts of artificial colors and preservatives.

Dog treats come in every size, shape and flavor imaginable, from organic cookies shaped like postmen to beefy chew sticks. Dogs seem to love them all, so enjoy the variety. Just be sure not to overindulge your dog. Factor treats into her regular meal sizes.

*Proper nutri-
tion is neces-
sary for the
overall health
and good looks
of your Akita.*

seems unnecessary with the availability of so many high-quality commercially prepared dog foods.

The Role of Enzymes

In nature animals know to seek out those foods that satisfy their nutritional needs. Assuming archeologists are correct and dogs are descended from wolves, we must examine wolf behavior to properly provide for our dogs. Free-roaming wolves hunt grazing animals whenever possible. Before eating muscle and bone, the pack feasts on the liver, pancreas, stomach contents, intestines and other internal organs. These organs provide an immediate supply of digestive enzymes while providing important vitamins and minerals that came from the vegetation eaten by their prey.

When puppies are weaned and waiting at the den for dinner, they are fed regurgitated food high in digestive enzymes. During those lean times when grazing animals are not readily available, a hungry wolf eats small rodents, which contain digestive enzymes in proportion to the meal.

Domestic dogs are fed processed food minus digestive enzymes. Compounding the problem, chlorine used to purify water and fluoride found in many municipal water supplies prevent the body from producing adequate amounts of digestive enzymes.

You can provide this vital supplement, which is available at your health food store in capsule form. One capsule per meal will assist in digestion and assimilation. Be sure it contains ox bile, pancreatin, pepsin, bromelain, betaine and papain. Puppies also benefit from a digestive enzyme supplement.

Additives in Dog Foods

Wolves also eat herbs and other plants found in their natural habitat. Dogs in their natural habitat (our homes) feed on soybeans, by-products, propylene glycol, BHT, BHA, ethoxyquin, salt, sugar, chemicals, preservatives, food dyes and other unhealthy substances included in dog food. Is it any wonder that our dogs suffer from bloat, thyroid disease, cancer and skin/coat problems, when you consider the array of additives they commonly ingest by eating popular supermarket dog foods or too much human food?

Snack-type dog biscuits available in supermarkets also contain ingredients that are known to be harmful. For example, a popular brand of dog biscuits contains (among other chemicals) monosodium glutamate, a chemical associated with brain damage in babies and recently re-moved from commercial baby foods.

Some dry dog foods may also contain harmful additives. An ingredient now added to many dry dog foods is ethoxyquin, a fat preservative. Controversy over the safety of this product has increased in recent years. Breeders of purebred dogs blame health, reproductive and birth defect problems on the addition of ethoxyquin to commercial dog foods. Although the manufacturers of the additive, and those dog food companies that include it in their recipes, claim it is safe, research with rats has linked the additive to kidney cancer.

HOW TO READ THE DOG FOOD LABEL

With so many choices on the market, how can you be sure you are feeding the right food for your dog? The information is all there on the label—if you know what you're looking for.

Look for the nutritional claim right up top. Is the food "100% nutritionally complete"? If so, it's for nearly all life stages; "growth and maintenance," on the other hand, is for early development; puppy foods are marked as such, as are foods for senior dogs.

Ingredients are listed in descending order by weight. The first three or four ingredients will tell you the bulk of what the food contains. Look for the highest-quality ingredients, like meats and grains, to be among them.

The Guaranteed Analysis tells you what levels of protein, fat, fiber and moisture are in the food, in that order. While these numbers are meaningful, they won't tell you much about the quality of the food. Nutritional value is in the dry matter, not the moisture content.

In many ways, seeing is believing. If your dog has bright eyes, a shiny coat, a good appetite and a good energy level, chances are his diet's fine. Your dog's breeder and your veterinarian are good sources of advice if you're still confused.

BHT and BHA are preservatives found in many dog foods, but these additives are associated with immune system suppression, decreased white blood cells and some cancers. Look for foods with natural preservatives such as vitamins C and E. Yes, these foods have a shorter shelf life, but chemicals shorten the life of your dog.

Food Possessiveness

Before proceeding with a suggested schedule, the following message is one of the most important in this book, because Akitas are food possessive. From the first day your puppy begins his life with you, have family members take turns removing his food bowl during mealtime. Hold the bowl up, out of reach for a moment, then replace the bowl and allow the puppy to continue eating. Do this at intervals, not necessarily daily, just to get him used to having family members take things from him. Do the same thing with a favorite toy, a chew bone, a snack cookie.

On other occasions while he is eating, add more food to the bowl—a piece of meat, a spoonful of cottage cheese, something he particularly likes. Akitas are frequently possessive about food and toys; whether they intend eating them or not, they do not want to share. Getting the puppy used to having your fingers in his bowl while he is eating is insurance that he won't, someday, mistake your fingers for food. This training may also prove worthwhile if your adult Akita gets hold of something poisonous and you *have* to get it away quickly.

Going Off Puppy Food

Large breeds like the Akita do not require puppy food after the age of four months. The higher protein found in commercial puppy foods promotes rapid growth, and with it comes developmental problems. A premium dry dog food is ideal for puppies, providing sufficient easily digested protein to achieve expected growth, without causing skeletal problems associated with an abnormally rapid growth pattern.

Puppies up to the age of six months may be fed three meals a day. If your puppy is becoming too round and fat, cut back to two meals—you do not want too much weight on those soft, growing bones. Once a dog reaches six months of age, and for the balance of the dog's life, he should be fed twice a day, at least nine hours or more apart.

Your dog's diet will vary depending on how old and how active he is. This dog is competing in obedience.

How Much to Feed

The amount to feed each dog depends upon the dog himself. For example, active dogs will require more food than sedentary dogs, and lactating bitches need more food than normal adult bitches. Most Akitas do not eat (or need) massive amounts of food. The average adult Akita maintains a good weight on two to three cups of dry food, twice daily, with a few snack cookies between meals.

To determine the amount of food your puppy or adult Akita requires, start by feeding one-and-a-half cups of food per meal. If the dog leaves some and walks away, then cut back to an amount of food eaten within ten minutes. You do not want your dog to be too thin or too fat. You should be able to feel the ribs and spine with your hand, but the skeleton should not be visible to the naked eye.

Should You Supplement?

Some veterinarians and breeders recommend supplementing with calcium and some do not. Veterinary studies have shown that excessive calcium can cause serious problems in growing dogs, particularly large breeds like the Akita. Skeletal diseases (like hip dysplasia), Marie's disease (where uneven and irregular bone deposits cause swelling of the soft tissue and thickening of joint capsules), osteochrondrosis dissecans (persistent lameness caused by thickening cartilage and lesions in the surface of the cartilage) and wobbler syndrome (malformation of cervical vertebrae resulting in spinal cord compression) are all associated with overfeeding and oversupplementing.

> ## TO SUPPLEMENT OR NOT TO SUPPLEMENT?
>
> If you're feeding your dog a diet that's correct for her developmental stage and she's alert, healthy-looking and neither over- nor underweight, you don't need to add supplements. These include table scraps as well as vitamins and minerals. In fact, a growing puppy is in danger of developing musculoskeletal disorders by oversupplementation. If you have any concerns about the nutritional quality of the food you're feeding, discuss them with your veterinarian.

Adding dairy products to your puppy's food will give him the proper ratio of the right forms of calcium. A few times weekly, add small amounts of grated cheeses, cottage cheese or yogurt, a hard-boiled egg and some ground beef or ground lamb.

The Akita thyroid gland produces only a third of necessary iodine. Therefore, the addition of a natural, easily assimilated iodine is important for an Akita. Most dog foods contain iodine as an additive, but much of it is dissipated during food processing. An excellent and inexpensive source of this natural iodine is kelp. Kelp is a seaweed that contains vitamins and twenty-two trace minerals. It comes in either powder or tablets or in combination with other sea plants and is available at pet supply stores and nutrition centers. Again, follow the directions on the label for the correct amounts to feed your dog.

Another important natural element added to most dog foods, but dissipated during food processing, is zinc. Zinc is necessary for proper growth, protein synthesis, immune function and reproduction. Some idiopathic skin/coat problems in Akitas respond well to zinc supplementation. Chelated zinc is the easiest form to assimilate—one 30mg tablet daily is recommended.

To cover your bases, add a multiple vitamin to the daily diet and one 8,000 to 10,000 IU softgel of vitamin A from fish oil. Vitamin A is the master cell builder necessary for development and maintenance of skin, coat, eyesight and proper immune function. Scientific research continues to discover important new areas where vitamin A is necessary, especially for cancer prevention.

Another food supplement that can be helpful under certain circumstances is gelatin. If you have a young dog with splayed feet, the problem may be nutritional. Between the ages of four and six months a puppy begins to get his adult teeth. At this time he is growing rapidly in size, and his ears are beginning to firm up. All these changes may lead to splayed feet, which can be corrected in some young puppies by adding a packet of unflavored gelatin to his food daily, for six weeks. Gelatin is a protein that may help the feet resume their correct form if the splaying is a result of nutritional deficits caused by rapid growth. If the splaying is genetic, however, gelatin will not help.

> **HOW MANY MEALS A DAY?**
>
> Individual dogs vary in how much they should eat to maintain a desired body weight—not too fat, but not too thin. Puppies need several meals a day, while older dogs may need only one. Determine how much food keeps your adult dog looking and feeling her best. Then decide how many meals you want to feed with that amount. Like us, most dogs love to eat, and offering two meals a day is more enjoyable for them. If you're worried about overfeeding, make sure you measure correctly and abstain from adding tidbits to the meals.
>
> Whether you feed one or two meals, only leave your dog's food out for the amount of time it takes her to eat it—10 minutes, for example. Freefooding (when food is available any time) and leisurely meals encourage picky eating. Don't worry if your dog doesn't finish all her dinner in the allotted time. She'll learn she should.

Many people add corn oil or some other type of oil to their puppy's food without realizing that oil can interfere with assimilation of other supplements. If your puppy is receiving a good-quality dog food with adequate amounts of fat, there is no reason to add oil.

Oil supplements are helpful only when there is a skin problem indicative of a fat deficiency. If your dog is suffering from dry skin which is not related to thyroid dysfunction, then oil might be considered. For dry skin, bacon grease, pork fat, or avocados are effective fat supplements.

Flavoring and Scraps

Now that you have gone to all the trouble to find the perfect food, then filled a cupboard with vitamin supplements, you need to make sure your Akita will eat what you serve. If you add a few tablespoons of canned food for flavoring, at least a half cup of warm water and stir everything well, your Akita will gobble up every morsel. As often as once or twice a week you can substitute canned or fresh fish for the canned dog food. Mackerel, salmon or tuna will delight your Akita.

You can add table scraps as often as you wish, but avoid gas-producing foods like cabbage. Onions are believed to cause anemia in dogs and should be avoided. Cooked whole grains like brown rice, oats and millet are very healthful additions.

At each meal, add a tablespoon of plain yogurt. Besides being a high-quality protein and source of calcium, yogurt contains bacterial cultures beneficial to the intestines, and they inhibit the growth of bacteria that breed toxins. It is an excellent food. If your dog has been receiving antibiotics for any reason, the addition of yogurt to the diet will replenish the beneficial intestinal flora destroyed by the antibiotic; these flora are necessary for assimilation and proper digestion.

Eggs are also very good for your Akita, but they must be cooked. Raw egg white contains a substance called avidin that binds to biotin, an essential B vitamin, interfering with its absorption. Offer your dog a hard-boiled egg once or twice a week.

Holiday Health Alerts

On holidays, avoid feeding too much turkey and/or chicken skin or roast beef. An overabundance of these items will frequently cause diarrhea. During holidays, many people stock up on chocolates to serve their guests, but always keep chocolate away from your Akita. Chocolate contains theobromine, which acts as a toxin in large amounts, causing elevated blood pressure, vomiting, seizures and cardiac arrest.

For those dogs who enjoy raw fruit, like peaches, grapes or watermelon, there is no harm in allowing the dog to enjoy them in moderation. Be sure to remove any fruit pits before feeding. Vegetables, raw or cooked, can be given if they meet with your Akita's approval. Carrots are a good choice for teething puppies or a chew for an adult dog.

Changing Foods

Finally, if you are planning to switch foods, do so slowly. Over the course of a week or more, gradually reduce the amount of the old food while increasing the new food until the switch is completed. Sudden changes can cause digestive upsets and diarrhea.

Be vigilant in monitoring your dog's weight. When you notice a little too much fat forming around your Akita's midsection, reduce the dog's food intake by at least 25 percent. To accomplish food reduction and still prevent hunger, replace the amount of withheld food with canned vegetables like green beans, asparagus or carrots. Other options are to use a lower-calorie food, or switch to one of the specially formulated reducing diets. You should discuss this with your veterinarian before making any major changes in the dog's diet. During any reducing diet, you must eliminate all treats and snacks.

Rather than periodic reducing diets for your Akita, you may prefer to switch your dog's diet altogether to one of the new light dog foods formulated especially for the older and less active dog. These foods have a lower protein and fat content but are nutritionally complete.

Feeding Older Dogs

As well as needing less fat in their diets, older inactive dogs do not require the same amount of protein as young dogs; besides which, large amounts of protein may contribute to kidney damage. Nearly all the large dog food manufacturers have come out with a line of light foods. Read the labels and make your selection.

When Your Dog Won't Eat

Sometimes your Akita may refrain from eating of his own accord. If this happens, be careful to ascertain the cause. During the teething stages, a puppy may turn away from a few meals. Usually this is caused by sore gums. You can give him an ice cube or two to dull the pain enough to restore his appetite. Using a baby teething gel on the gums also can bring relief. When an adult Akita stops eating, it may be a sign of impending illness. If, however, the dog appears healthy and will take a snack treat, it could just be the onset of "let's be finicky and drive the owner crazy" syndrome. Wait a day to see if his appetite picks up. If loss of appetite continues, seek veterinary attention.

A Need to Chew

Opinion is divided on whether or not to give beef bones to dogs. Some veterinarians do not recommend beef bones because they can break off and splinter, causing intestinal damage. They can also damage and weaken tooth enamel. A good alternative to beef bones is rawhide bones, which now come in all sizes, shapes and designs. Flavored chews made from a strong, long-lasting material also satisfy the need to chew and are perfectly safe. Carrots are excellent for chewing and may be frozen for the teething puppy. You can discuss this with your veterinarian before making a decision.

I prefer to give my Akitas chopped and formed rawhide chews. With the chopped and formed chews, the chances of the dog choking on a large piece of rawhide are small, yet these chews are still tough enough to give their teeth and gums a thorough workout. This form of rawhide treat is excellent for the older dog who may have suffered some tooth loss.

chapter 6

Grooming
Your
Akita

Compared to many medium-to long-haired breeds, Akitas are a pleasure to groom. Their resilient, odorless coats require no special trimming and a regular weekly brushing is all that is necessary to keep them naturally beautiful. Beyond this, the Akita's grooming needs are the same as one would expect for short-haired breeds.

There are many advantages to using a professional groomer. The indoor facility allows bathing throughout the year; groomers use a high-power blow-dryer to remove dead hair and, for a reasonable price, your dog is returned to you smelling like an expensive cologne. Ask your veterinarian to recommend a reliable groomer.

Trimming Your Dog's Nails

Your Akita's nails are too long if they touch the floor when she is walking. If you hear a continuous "click-click," it is time to cut the nails. If the dog spends time

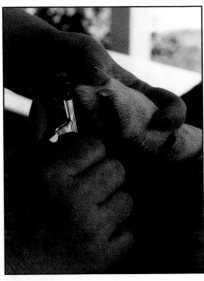

on concrete, the nails may be worn down by constant contact with the rough surface. But if your yard is grass and your Akita never walks on hard surfaces, her nails will require periodic trimming. Older Akitas require more regular attention to the nails. As the dog slows down with age, she will not keep her nails naturally short, and the longer nails will inhibit her ability to walk.

A few Akitas are indifferent to nail trimming, but most dislike the process entirely. Because of this, start trimming when they are

If you get your Akita used to it at a young age, he will tolerate the necessary procedure of having his nails clipped.

puppies and they will be used to it when they are large enough to pull away from you. Purchase a sturdy nail trimmer that can sever thick nails quickly and with a minimum of effort. Begin by cutting off small pieces at the edge. With nearly clear (light pigmented) nails, check to see exactly where the blood vessels are by shining a small flashlight through the nail. Then continue cutting until you've reached the desired length, staying away from the end of the vein (the quick).

Trim the nail to a point just in front of the quick. If in doubt, take off very little. If you accidentally draw blood, a styptic pencil or powder will stop the bleeding. If you are dealing with very long nails, you might want to consider using an electric grinder. Grinders are effective in reducing nail length slowly. The drawback to this method is that your Akita will have to become accustomed to the noise of the tool, and it will be necessary for you to grind the nails back a little at a time, and on a frequent and consistent basis. Each time you grind the nails, veins will recede farther back; eventually, it will be easier to maintain your Akita's short nails.

Though Akitas don't need extra-special grooming, they do have thick coats that shed occasionally.

If you have any concerns about what you are doing or are afraid of hurting your Akita, you may prefer to have your veterinarian do the job or at least show you the proper way.

Combing and Brushing

Twice a year, Akitas blow out (lose) their undercoat and grow a new one. It is a messy process and they look unkempt and shaggy while "blowing," but a daily combing with a metal comb or brushing with a pin brush assists in removing the dead fur. If the weather is warm, a bath in warm water will also promote the blow and hasten the process to completion. When they are not blowing, Akitas shed very little. Before bathing your dog, spend time brushing to remove dead fur.

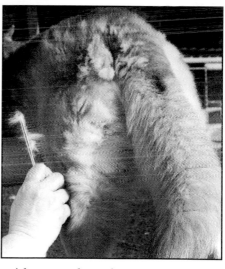

This dog is "blowing" coat, which is why clumps of fur are sticking out.

61

Bathing Your Akita

Healthy skin begins with a healthy diet, but good grooming is an important adjunct. If you plan to bathe your Akita at home, give some thought to where a shaking, wet dog will do the least damage. A shower stall is a possibility if it is large enough to accommodate you and your Akita. The bathtub is ideal because the Akita goes inside the tub and you remain reasonably dry outside the tub. In either case, provide a nonslip surface like a rubber shower mat.

It takes a lot of shampoo and water to penetrate the Akita's double coat. You can expect to get wet in the process.

GROOMING TOOLS

pin brush

slicker brush

flea comb

towel

mat rake

grooming glove

scissors

nail clippers

tooth-cleaning equipment

shampoo

conditioner

clippers

If your kitchen has a window not too far from an appropriate bathing area, you can attach a hose to the kitchen sink. The necessary hardware coupling is available at hardware stores. During flea season, use an herbal flea shampoo or one with pyrethrum (refer to chapter 7). White or pinto Akitas benefit from a whitening shampoo, available at your pet supply store. Use one of the canine tearless shampoos to wash her face.

The Akita's double coat is difficult to penetrate. Wet the fur to the skin and shampoo into a lather. Keep water from running into the ears by holding the earflap forward to rinse. Thoroughly rinse all soap from the coat; any remaining soap will cause itching. After the rinse, use a clean washcloth to gently wipe the eyes clear of water and towel dry with bath towels.

Before and during the bath, look for dry, dull coat, flaking skin, bald spots or sores: They can be signs of a developing health problem, a flea allergy or a food allergy. As you lather, check your Akita for lumps, bumps and warts. Cysts and other growths are common in older dogs and should be monitored by your veterinarian and removed if necessary.

A well-groomed dog looks great and feels great.

Elbow Calluses

If your Akita spends a large amount of time reclining on a hard surface, you may notice her elbows forming a hard callus. This is a natural protection provided by nature as a cushion. Keep an eye on these elbow calluses and apply some lanolin or dry-skin cream to the callus if you notice signs of cracking. In some cases, an infection can begin under the hardened skin. These require immediate veterinary attention.

chapter 7

Keeping Your
Akita
Healthy

The overall health of your Akita depends on the teamwork between you and your veterinarian, which is why it's crucial to have a good vet. If you already have a veterinarian you can trust, great. If not, how do you find one?

One of the best ways is by referral. Ask an Akita breeder for a recommendation. One of the best sources for vets knowledgeable about your breed are the people who rescue Akitas. (People who "rescue" particular breeds take the dogs from shelters or owners who can no longer keep them and find new homes for the dogs.) People who rescue Akitas work with vets who are already experts on the breed simply by the sheer numbers of Akitas brought in for care and treatment. You can also call the American Animal Hospital Association in Colorado (303) 279-2500 and ask for a listing in your area. AAHA members must keep and maintain clean, well-equipped hospitals.

Your Puppy's Shots

During the first twenty-four hours of his life a puppy receives antibodies through the process of nursing. Antibodies are molecules produced by the immune system to fight the "enemy" diseases. The degree of protection a puppy receives depends on the mother's antibody level when the puppy was born. If the mother has been vaccinated a few months before giving birth, she should have high levels of protective antibodies. These maternal antibodies can last for up to sixteen weeks in the puppy's system.

After the maternal antibodies have lost their effectiveness, your puppy will need vaccinations to help build his own antibodies. A series of puppy vaccines given either singly or in combination are required to induce immunity against the following contagious diseases.

YOUR PUPPY'S VACCINES

Vaccines are given to prevent your dog from getting an infectious disease like canine distemper or rabies. Vaccines are the ultimate preventive medicine: they're given before your dog ever gets the disease so as to protect him from the disease. That's why it is necessary for your dog to be vaccinated routinely. Puppy vaccines start at eight weeks of age for the five-in-one DHLPP vaccine and are given every three to four weeks until the puppy is sixteen months old. Your veterinarian will put your puppy on a proper schedule and will remind you when to bring in your dog for shots.

Distemper is a highly contagious viral disease, often fatal to puppies.

Parvovirus is a relatively new and very serious disease. Puppies are especially susceptible to this contagious disease—many die within hours after exhibiting symptoms.

Canine hepatitis is an infectious viral disease. It is unrelated to human hepatitis.

Leptospirosis is carried predominantly by rats.

Parainfluenza is a communicable disease that affects the respiratory system, causing a harsh, dry cough and nasal discharge. In puppies, it is more serious than in adult dogs. Treatment is usually effective with antibiotics, cough suppressants and rest.

ADVANTAGES OF SPAY/NEUTER

The greatest advantage of spaying (for females) or neutering (for males) your dog is that you are guaranteed your dog will not produce puppies. There are too many puppies already available for too few homes. There are other advantages as well.

ADVANTAGES OF SPAYING

No messy heats.

No "suitors" howling at your windows or waiting in your yard.

Decreased incidences of pyometra (disease of the uterus) and breast cancer.

ADVANTAGES OF NEUTERING

Lessens male aggressive and territorial behaviors, but doesn't affect the dog's personality. Behaviors are often owner-induced, so neutering is not the only answer, but it is a good start.

Prevents the need to roam in search of bitches in season.

Decreased incidences of urogenital diseases.

Coronavirus is often mistaken for parvovirus, but one important difference is coronavirus is usually responsive to treatment and rarely fatal.

The **rabies** vaccine is usually not given until a dog is at least four months of age. In many states, a rabies vaccination is mandatory. Ask your veterinarian about the requirements in your state.

Spaying or Neutering

There are several advantages to spaying your bitch or neutering your dog, but first let us review some of the myths.

MYTHS VS. FACTS

Myth: Spayed and neutered animals gain weight simply because they are surgically sterilized. *Fact:* Overeating, lack of exercise and thyroid problems are the real causes of weight gain.

Myth: Dogs between the ages of six months and one year require sexual hormones for normal growth. *Fact:* Growth is not determined by the testicles or ovaries, but by the pituitary gland.

Myth: Female dogs require at least one litter of puppies to make them well-adjusted. *Fact:* Good temperament is not dependent on the experience of motherhood; genetics, socialization and human/animal bonding are responsible for temperament and self-confidence.

Myth: Masculinity is diminished by removal of the dog's testicles. *Fact:* Masculine traits are programmed at conception in much the same way nature selects color schemes and genetic diseases.

PHYSICAL BENEFITS

Unspayed female dogs are frequent victims of pyometra, a dangerous, potentially fatal uterine infection that can be costly to treat. By removing the uterus you remove the possibility of pyometra as well as of uterine and ovarian cancers. Females spayed before the age of one year also have a significantly lower incidence of mammary cancer, which generally occurs in unspayed female dogs six years or older.

There are many health benefits to spaying or neutering your Akita; neutered animals can still compete in obedience.

These tumors frequently occur after a heat cycle, and are usually malignant. Female dogs spayed during the first year of life rarely develop breast cancer. The best time to spay your female is before she reaches sexual maturity by the seventh or eighth month.

Neutering a male dog at an early age prevents behavioral problems, including fighting, urine marking and overt aggression. Testicles produce the hormone testosterone, which is thought to be responsible for some forms of territorial aggression. Dogs neutered at five months of age, before the production of testosterone begins, are often far less aggressive as adults.

The incidence of prostate infections and prostate cancer, hernias and testicular tumors are greatly reduced in neutered males. Prostate gland enlargement and/or infection is one of the more common problems in an intact male dog, and may lead to kidney problems. This potentially serious and always painful condition may require neutering in the older dog; and any surgery in an older dog is more dangerous than in a younger one.

External Parasites

FLEAS

How do you know if your Akita has fleas? The dog's behavior—constant scratching and chewing—are noticeable signs of fleas, and can tip you off. Also, separate the fur to look for flea "debris," small black specks resembling ground pepper, especially around the base of the tail, the stomach and inner thighs. These black dots are flea feces that dissolve into residual blood when dropped into water. The blood is from your dog, the waste products of fleas feeding on your Akita. If you watch patiently, you will catch a fleeting glimpse of a flea on the run.

It is difficult to control fleas completely in warm climates. For those living in warm, coastal areas, fleas are a year-round problem, and residents are usually experts on fleas. Yard spraying is easy if you have a small property. But just take your dog for a walk in a nearby park or field and you have flea infestation all over again.

Periodic flea baths and flea sprays combined with control measures in the dog's environment are one means of control. Flea collars don't usually work; fleas simply avoid the neck area or jump over the collar. Some dogs even develop a dermatitis underneath the flea collar. If you use a collar, you should periodically remove it to check for skin irritation. In the meantime, we should all pray that scientists find an easy way to solve the flea problem—soon.

FIGHTING FLEAS

Remember, the fleas you see on your dog are only part of the problem—the smallest part! To rid your dog and home of fleas, you need to treat your dog *and* your home. Here's how:

• Identify where your pet(s) sleep. These are "hot spots."

• Clean your pets' bedding regularly by vacuuming and washing.

• Spray "hot spots" with a non-toxic, long-lasting flea larvicide.

• Treat outdoor "hot spots" with insecticide.

• Kill eggs on pets with a product containing insect growth regulators (IGRs).

• Kill fleas on pets per your veterinarian's recommendation.

There are many sprays and insecticides on the market to attack fleas during all phases of this parasite's life cycle. This cycle may appear endless, but the egg-to-larvae-to-adult process is only three to six weeks. To break this cycle you must attack fleas where they reside: on your dog, in your house, and in your yard. Keep in mind that if you are using one type of spray on your dog,

another type in your home and yet a third type in your yard, you may be setting up a toxic living environment for you and your Akita. Any chemical designed to kill fleas is toxic, but the least toxic chemical for use against fleas is pyrethrum. Pyrethrum is derived from the African chrysanthemum. (Pyrethrin is the synthetic form of pyrethrum.) It must be used consistently since its effectiveness is not as lasting as more toxic chemicals. Many sprays with pyrethrum or pyrethrin also include an insect growth inhibitor that is not toxic to children or pets.

Eradicating adult fleas does not end the problem. Even when most of the adult fleas have been destroyed, new fleas will continue to develop from the eggs and larvae a few weeks later. Repeated spraying is necessary to continue killing fleas. Because of the time, effort and work involved in flea control, some dog owners prefer to use a professional exterminator.

Another option for you to discuss with your veterinarian is an internal once-a-month drug that breaks the flea cycle by inhibiting normal formation of chitin, the hard outer shell encasing the flea. Without the hard protective covering, flea larvae cannot develop.

*The flea is a
die-hard pest.*

*To keep fleas
under control,
treat your dog,
house and yard,
and check your
puppy whenever
he comes inside.*

A combination of natural, nontoxic products will provide adequate flea control if you begin before the onset of official flea season. With the first crocus, begin spraying your yard with nematodes, infinitesimal insects genetically programmed to eat flea eggs and larvae. These harmless insects begin working within twenty-four hours, then effectively clean up after fleas for four weeks. Reapply the mixture monthly throughout flea season for good environmental control. Inside your home a boron-based powder or crystals applied to the carpet will kill flea larvae for months, or you can use an insect growth regulator widely available in sprays and foggers. Topping off your nontoxic flea program, diatomaceous earth (DE), a one-celled plant mined from the ocean and ground into a fine particle dust, is applied to your dog's skin (use only chemical-free "natural grade" DE).

After many years as a flea warrior in a warm climate, I have discovered a perfect method of DE application without creating a cloud of dust. Remove the foot from a worn pair of panty hose, fill with DE, knot at the top and use this as an applicator. Rub the DE close to the skin, starting at the neck and working down. Avoid inhaling the dust and keep it away from the dog's eyes. Repeat weekly. The diatoms clog the fleas' breathing and pierce the hard shell, killing the adult fleas within twelve to thirty-six hours.

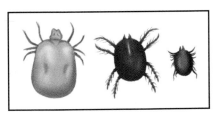

Three types of ticks (l-r): the wood tick, brown dog tick and deer tick.

TICKS

Ticks can be found in all parts of North America. In cold areas they are dormant during winter months, but in warm areas they thrive year-round. These small insects are flat when not feeding, but swell to large proportions when engorged with your dog's blood. These disgusting creatures carry serious diseases, including Lyme disease (symptoms are fever, loss of appetite, enlarged lymph nodes and arthritis), Rocky Mountain Spotted Fever, ehrlichiosis and babesiosis. After a hike through a tick-infested area, you should check your dog (and yourself) for ticks and remove any you see.

The head, neck, ears, around the eyes and the feet are the most common sites to find ticks on your dog, but they can be hiding almost anywhere. A good insect repellent rubbed on the inside flaps of the ears will usually keep ticks from that area. A light spraying on the feet, chest and stomach with either a repellent or an insecticide will help keep them off the rest of your dog. Spray just before heading into tick country.

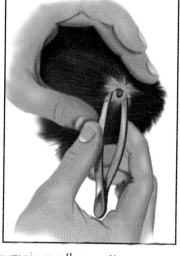

If you find yourself faced with the unpleasant task of removing ticks from your dog, saturate the exposed tick with alcohol, then use your fingers or a tweezer to grasp the engorged tick firmly. Twist and pull gently until it comes out. Apply some alcohol to the area. The site will often remain swollen and hard for a week. Ticks are difficult to destroy after removing them from your dog; flush them down the toilet or burn them. *Note:* After touching ticks, wash your hands carefully.

Use tweezers to remove ticks from your dog.

Mange has become an increasing problem in some areas of the country where the warm climate is an ideal breeding ground for mites, fleas and other parasites. Mange is caused by a mite that burrows under the dog's skin and sets up housekeeping. If not treated, the disease spreads. It is contagious only through direct contact with the mites. Symptoms of mange include loss of fur, severe itching, a strong musky odor and crustlike formations on the skin. There are many effective treatments for these pesky bugs.

Internal Parasites

HEARTWORM

Warm weather brings with it a grave danger to animals—heartworms—that live and grow in the dog's bloodstream, lodging in the heart and lungs. These parasites do irreparable damage before symptoms are evident, which is usually not until the disease has advanced. Heartworms are transmitted by infected mosquitoes. Treatment for heartworm can be just as dangerous as the heartworms; fortunately, heartworm can be prevented. Set aside time to discuss heartworm with your veterinarian. He/she will be able to advise you about heartworm infestation in your area, and will discuss the preventive drugs with you.

OTHER WORMS

Puppies are more susceptible to intestinal parasites than adult dogs. **Roundworms, hookworms,** and **whipworms** are more life-threatening to

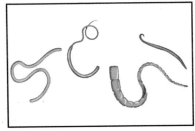

Common internal parasites (l-r): roundworm, whipworm, tapeworm and hookworm.

puppies. Your veterinarian will test a stool sample to determine the presence of these parasites. There are many safe and effective worm medications to treat these parasites. It should also be pointed out that the larvae of intestinal worms can migrate to human children when a child ingests soil contaminated with worm eggs. **Tapeworms** are carried by the flea and infect dogs when they bite and swallow the flea or when they hunt and eat a flea-infested animal.

If your dog has a history of periodic stomach and/or intestinal upsets, you should have your veterinarian test for **giardiasis,** a protozoan that has become epidemic in some areas of the country. Giardia can infect your dog through contact with contaminated feces or when the giardia cysts are washed into waterways by rainfall and melting snow.

Overall Care

EAR CARE

Some Akitas are more prone to ear infections as they grow older. Keeping the ears clean helps in prevention. To do this, use a soft, dampened facecloth, and gently clean out the external part of the ear. To remove the wax accumulations inside the ear, regularly use a disinfectant ear cleaning solution available through your veterinarian or at pet supply stores. Apply a liberal amount of the solution into the ear canal, then gently massage the base of the ear for a few minutes. Use a sterile pad of cotton inserted into the canal to remove the liquid.

It is normal for a dog to shake his head immediately after his ears have been cleansed. During the ear cleaning procedure, smell the inside of the ear. If you detect a musky, foul or strong odor, it could suggest an infection, and you should make an appointment to have it checked by your veterinarian.

CARING FOR EYES

Serious eye problems can develop in an older dog. Although it is normal for an older dog to have a slight clouding look to the lens, you should pay close attention to your Akita's eyes, since glaucoma and progressive retinal atrophy are to be found in this breed. Watch for abnormal symptoms like loss of vision (including night blindness), enlargement of one or both eyes, reddened eyelids, excessive tearing and pus. Your veterinarian should check your dog's eyes during routine physicals.

Make it a habit to check your dog's ears, eyes and teeth for anything unusual-looking.

KEEPING TEETH CLEAN

Like people, older dogs suffer from periodontal disease caused by a buildup of plaque and tartar. Indications of possible periodontal problems include mouth odor and loss of appetite. Each dog has a genetic code that dictates a tendency toward greater or lesser tartar buildup. You can regularly use a tooth-brush with dog toothpaste to brush your Akita's teeth. Products formulated especially for dogs can be found at the pet store.

Once tartar is present, it can only be removed by professional dental scaling, and this must be done under anesthesia. Keep a close watch on the condition of your Akita's teeth and gums. Scrape your fingernail along the surface of one large tooth. If your nail picks up a small amount of matter, it is an indication that plaque is present. Hard baked kibbles and rawhide chews also help in prevention.

Preventive Care

Akitas, given proper care and nutrition, are hearty. But even the strongest Akita can be susceptible to some of the same health problems as other breeds. Hopefully, your Akita will enjoy a lifetime free of serious illness. It helps, however, to know what problems could occur, how to recognize them and what treatment is necessary. Look for these signs of illness:

Loss of appetite

Vomiting/diarrhea

Excessive thirst

Rapid or slow pulse

Temperature under 100 or over 103 degrees Fahrenheit

Runny eyes

Unusual lethargy or restlessness

Coughing/sneezing

Behavior changes

TEMPERATURE

A dog's normal body temperature is 101 to 103 degrees Fahrenheit. When you need to take a temperature reading, try a digital read-out thermometer. Coat the tip of the thermometer with petroleum jelly and insert gently into the rectum about one-half inch. A beeper will sound when the thermometer is ready for a reading. Clean the thermometer after each use.

PULSE

A pulse reading tells you the frequency of heartbeats. Depending on the size of your Akita, the normal resting rate is between 60 to 150 beats per minute. The larger Akitas will have a slower rate. A pulse below 60 or over 180 beats per minute warrants a visit to the veterinarian. To take the pulse, locate the femoral artery. It's situated under the skin of the hind limb at the groin. Place the tips of your first and second fingers on the artery. Press and release the pressure on the artery until you feel a strong pulse. Count the beats for one minute.

BEHAVIOR

To give a pill, open the mouth wide, then drop it in the back of the throat

Be alert to your dog's normal behavior. Note any change in eating, or increased frequency in bowel and urinary patterns. Signs of illness include pain and/or discharge from the eyes or nose, coughing, excessive sneezing, labored or difficult breathing, drooling, excessive water consumption, vomiting and diarrhea, abnormal swellings, lameness or collapse. You should have on hand at least one book on basic dog care (see Chapter 3 for recommendations).

Giving Medicine

Medicating your dog can be easy if you follow one simple rule: disguise it. When **giving a pill** use a cheese spread, peanut butter, jelly, whipped cream, liverwurst or anything else suitable as a pill cover. Of course, you can give pills by prying the jaw open and dropping the pill behind the tongue. Time it so you can quickly close the dog's mouth, hold on as your Akita indignantly tries to escape, then rub his throat to encourage swallowing.

*Squeeze eye oint-
ment into the
lower lid.*

Giving **liquid medications** requires a syringe minus the needle, usually supplied with the medication. Insert the syringe in the side of the mouth and depress to release the liquid. Your Akita will allow you to accomplish the distasteful chore once but the next dose will tax your ingenuity. Speed is important as you reach down, grab the lip, insert the syringe and depress the plunger.

Itching

Sooner or later your Akita will begin chewing somewhere on his body. It's an inevitable fact when owning a dog. By process of elimination the word "allergy" will come up for discussion. **Allergies** do exist in the Akita; the problem is not uncommon. There are Akitas with flea allergies, food allergies and pollen allergies. If your dog has one small spot he has been chewing on, it does not necessarily follow that he is allergic to anything in particular.

Sometimes dogs will chew a "**hot spot**" simply from boredom or because it is very itchy from a flea bite. Effective home remedies are Desitin Baby Ointment that contains zinc oxide, A & D Ointment or Bag Balm Ointment, used for cows' udders. These are all water-repellent and have good adhering qualities that can keep them on the spot for days. The ointments soothe, heal and taste so terrible that most dogs will leave the area alone. Put a small amount on small cuts, insect bites and abrasions to relieve the discomfort.

If chewing persists for more than a few days, visit the veterinarian.

Diarrhea

Diarrhea is a symptom of something else. It could be a symptom of digestive upset, a chronic absorption disorder, a bacterial infection or an infectious disease process. If diarrhea occurs without other symptoms, assume it is caused by ingestion of some delicacy in your yard. Treat with an over-the-counter antidiarrheal medication like Kaopectate. For an adult dog, use half the recommended adult dose. Withhold food and water for twenty-four hours, then introduce a bland diet of cooked chicken or boiled ground beef and plain white rice. If the diarrhea continues, contact your veterinarian.

There are a few intestinal disorders found in Akitas. A trace of blood in the stool suggests colitis, an inflammation of the large bowel. It is a chronic problem controlled with proper diet and medication. Diarrhea in a puppy can be a serious problem because puppies rapidly dehydrate. Contact your veterinarian.

Vomiting

Vomiting is another symptom of an underlying cause. Vomiting or attempts to vomit are associated with bloat (see later in this chapter), a life-threatening emergency. Since vomiting is the purposeful expulsion of the stomach contents, it often occurs when a dog has eaten one of those strange backyard delicacies. Treat the Akita with Pepto-Bismol and withhold food and water for twelve hours. Feed a bland diet of cooked chicken or boiled ground beef and white rice. The problem should be resolved if it's a simple gastric upset. However, it can be a symptom of a more serious disease process and should not be ignored. If vomiting contains traces of blood, contact your veterinarian immediately. Again, puppies are prone to dehydration from vomiting and diarrhea; call your veterinarian.

Poisons

Seasonal changes mean seasonal **poison** dangers. During the summer months, be very careful with lawn fertilizers, herbicides and insecticides. In the winter months, remember that nearly all liquids used for automobile maintenance and repair, as well as salts for snow, are hazards. Topping the list is automotive antifreeze. Antifreeze attracts dogs with its sweet taste, but the results of ingestion are fatal.

Some of the many household substances harmful to your dog.

Other poisons found in the average home include pain relievers, medications of all types, all detergents, cleaners, polishers, hair products, gasoline, fungicides, herbicides, insecticides, rodent and snail poisons and cosmetics. Remember that any household product that can be both attractive and poisonous for your child is an equal hazard for a curious puppy. Puppy-proof and child-proof your home by storing these products in areas that are not accessible or in cupboards with locking latches.

Many household and outdoor **plants** can be fatal when ingested. For example, poinsettia, abundantly available during the holiday season, is toxic. The vine portions of potato and tomato plants, the tops of rhubarb, the leaves of avocado and peach trees are all poisonous to your Akita. If you think your Akita has eaten any of these things, give that information to your veterinarian. Do not induce vomiting until you have spoken with a medical professional.

Toadstools deserve special mention because they are found everywhere and in great variety. The poison from the mushroom acts like a snake venom, and even a small amount can be fatal. Remove toadstools from your yard after each rain.

Foxtails and grass awns also deserve special mention. Both can enter a dog's body by working through the skin or entering through any of a dog's body cavities, the nose and ears being the most common.

Flies are another problem. Usually, flies attack the tips of the dog's ears and can cause unsightly damage. Daily application of a fly repellent will solve the problem. During warm months, when flies are active, mix two-thirds insect repellent with one-third petroleum jelly and apply to the tips of the ears. You can greatly reduce the number of flies in your Akita's environment by picking up and properly discarding stools on a regular basis.

Akitas love snow and cold weather. These two are enjoying a romp.

Emergency First Aid

Nearly all cases involving emergency first aid will require transport to a veterinarian. To assist in providing the best medical care available for your dog, call ahead to the veterinary facility so they can make preparations for the emergency. Before an emergency occurs, consult with your veterinarian. Is the veterinary hospital staffed twenty-four hours a day? If not, is your veterinarian on call? If your veterinarian does not provide after-hours care, you will need an emergency pet hospital. Where is it located?

CANINE CPR

If your dog has stopped breathing there may not be sufficient time to transport the Akita to the closest open veterinary hospital without initiating cardiopulmonary resuscitation (CPR).

It is important to know the correct position of the heart for this treatment. On the dog's left side, flex the elbow joint against the body. The elbow tip is the approximate location of the heart. Have your veterinarian give you a demonstration of this procedure, but just in case you are using this book in an emergency, here's what you do: For puppies or Akitas under 50 pounds, roll the dog onto his back with head extended back. Kneel down at the head, place your palms on the chest slightly below the juncture of the arms. Clasp your fingers with the palms resting on either side of the chest. Using moderate pressure, compress your palms down on the chest for a count of "2" and release for a count of "1." Do this quickly, at least thirty times within thirty seconds.

Alternate with **artificial respiration** by breathing into the nostrils sufficiently to expand the chest for three seconds. For adult dogs or dogs over 50 pounds, roll the dog on his side with his spine facing you. Place the palm of your hand in the middle of the chest and begin compressions alternated with nostril breathing. Every few minutes, check to see if the heart has restarted. Once the heart is beating transport the dog to the veterinarian.

Use a scarf or old hose to make a temporary muzzle, as shown.

TYING A MUZZLE

Any injured dog may bite. To avoid being bitten, muzzle the dog before evaluating his condition or moving him to another area. Use whatever is at hand—a piece of rope, a necktie, a lady's stocking or a length of torn fabric. Loop the material around the closed muzzle at least twice, then tie a single knot under the chin. Bring the free ends back around the head below the ears and tie a bow. If a dog is choking, do *not* use a muzzle; it will close the remaining airway.

TRAUMA

If your Akita is injured in an auto accident or hit by an oncoming car, you must transport the dog to a veterinarian without causing further injury. A blanket makes an adequate stretcher with two people holding the four ends to keep it level. If you suspect a head or neck injury, a stiff board should be used to keep the head and neck from moving. Secure the dog to the board with rope or something similar and transport.

HEATSTROKE

This is an abnormally high body temperature caused by environmental heat. *Never* leave any dog in an unattended car unless the temperature outside is cold. The inside of a car on a moderately warm day will quickly reach insufferable temperatures. A dog left unattended with the windows up will quickly develop heatstroke, which is often fatal. Likewise, a dog left in an unshaded cement run may also suffer a debilitating rise in body temperature. Furthermore, older, out-of-shape Akitas suddenly subjected to strenuous exercise on a hot day can suffer heatstroke.

Symptoms of heatstroke are extreme panting, excessive salivation, vomiting and collapse. Any of these symptoms necessitate immediate veterinary care.

It is necessary to cool the body by immersing the dog in cold water or keeping a water hose running across his body. Start this procedure as someone calls the veterinarian. Apply ice packs to the dog as he's transported to the vet.

ELECTROCUTION

Puppies are curious by nature and prone to chew on any visible object, including electric cords. Electrical cords are a hazard to puppies allowed to roam freely in a home. Once the puppy bites into the cord and receives an initial shock, he may not be able to release the cord from his mouth. Severe **burns** and even **electrocution** can occur. If this should occur, do not touch the puppy. First disconnect the electric cord from the socket by using a wooden object. You can then touch the puppy without fear of electrocuting yourself.

A strong electrical shock can cause severe damage and may even stop the heart. If the dog is not breathing, cardiopulmonary resuscitation (CPR) must be initiated immediately (see above for instructions).

To prevent the tragedy of electrical shock, puppies should be supervised in the home and corrected when they approach electrical cords.

BLEEDING AND PUNCTURE WOUNDS

Of all wounds, the most dangerous is a severe bleeding injury, which can kill your dog in minutes unless you take action to control it. Use sterile dressings or a clean cloth to cover the wound, then apply continuous direct pressure to stop the flow of blood. Do not remove the dressing, since this will remove the protective layer of clotted blood and allow the wound to reopen. Maintain direct pressure as you transport the dog to your veterinarian. When no one is available to help you, apply sterile dressings to the wound, secure with a tightly wound gauze wrap and transport immediately.

Dog fights often result in puncture wounds, deep wounds with a small point of entry that tend to fester unless treated with antibiotics.

A FIRST-AID KIT

Keep a canine first-aid kit on hand for general care and emergencies. Check it periodically to make sure liquids haven't spilled or dried up, and replace medications and materials after they're used. Your kit should include:

Activated charcoal tablets

Adhesive tape
(1 and 2 inches wide)

Antibacterial ointment
(for skin and eyes)

Aspirin (buffered or enteric coated, *not* Ibuprofen)

Bandages: Gauze rolls (1 and 2 inches wide) and dressing pads

Cotton balls

Diarrhea medicine

Dosing syringe

Hydrogen peroxide (3%)

Petroleum jelly

Rectal thermometer

Rubber gloves

Rubbing alcohol

Scissors

Tourniquet

Towel

Tweezers

CHOKING

Pawing at the mouth, showing signs of obvious distress and a blue tongue are signs of choking. The harder your dog tries to breathe, the more he will panic until he reaches a state of unconsciousness. Anything a dog takes into his mouth can end up in his throat, especially a golf or tennis ball. Choking is another life-threatening emergency, but one you must begin to deal with on your own. There is no time to transport a choking dog to a veterinarian.

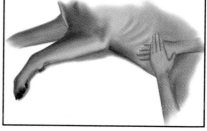

The goal of treatment is to open an airway without being bitten. Open the dog's mouth. If you can see the object you must decide if it can be removed with your fingers. The last thing you want to do is push it further into the airway. If you cannot pop it out easily or if the dog is unconscious the next step depends on your size and the size of your Akita. If size permits, hold the dog upside down by his rear legs and shake vigorously. If help is available, have them slap on the dog's back while you shake. This should dislodge the object.

Applying abdominal thrusts can save a choking dog.

If the dog is too large for this procedure use the abdom-inal compression method (**Heimlich maneuver**) to free the airway. Wrap your arms around the dog just behind the rib cage, your hands folded together into a tight fist on the abdominal area. Quickly thrust your arms back, compressing the abdomen. Sudden thrusts on the abdomen cause the diaphragm to bulge forward, forcing air and, hopefully, the object out of the windpipe. Try five or six compressions.

In either case, if the dog is not breathing, begin CPR and artificial respiration by blowing directly into the dog's nostrils to expand the chest. Transport to the hospital.

BROKEN BONES

A broken bone on a dog as large as an Akita requires immediate immobilization. In this case, pain is your ally because it prevents the dog from using the injured limb. Assess the extent of injury. If there is an open wound, do not apply a splint. Any break in the skin over the broken bone should be cleaned with a disinfectant like hydrogen peroxide to prevent infection. Cover with a folded bath towel and transport immediately.

Make a temporary splint by wrapping the leg in firm casing, then bandaging it.

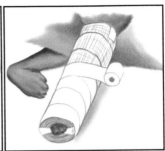

If the break is not open, here's your chance to invent a splint just like they do in the movies. Use rolled newspapers or magazines, PVC pipe or tree limbs—whatever is at hand. Attach the splint with tape or torn strips of fabric. Rig a sling with large bath towels by sliding one under the body to keep weight off the broken leg. Adjust the towels to accommodate either a broken front or hind limb. Once the Akita is settled into your vehicle, leave the makeshift sling in place until you reach your veterinarian.

Problems Particular to Akitas

Every breed of dog has genetic or inherited diseases, and Akitas are no exception. Akita breeders are just beginning to take steps toward improving the health of Akitas, but a number of diseases are now common in the breed.

HYPOTHYROIDISM

This is a disease that slowly destroys the thyroid gland's tissue over a period of years and leads to a reduction in the production of thyroid hormones. Symptoms of thyroid disease in an Akita vary with each animal and the dog may have more than one symptom. More often than not, a hypothyroid Akita will have skin and coat problems. Hot spots, dry flaky skin, dull broken coat, lack of coat, itching and chewing are all symptoms of the disease. Besides skin abnormalities, symptoms of hypothyroidism include behavior changes like sudden, unprovoked aggression, weight variations, seizures, and fatigue. An affected dog may show only one or two of the symptoms, or a combination of most or all.

A blood test will assist your veterinarian in diagnosing the disease. Most veterinary laboratories do limited thyroid tests to determine the amount of circulating hormone. New tests are gaining because they offer a more accurate assessment of thyroid function. One of these new tests is known as "equilibrium dialysis." It is available at veterinary teaching universities where your veterinarian can ship the blood sample. Thyroid disease cannot be cured, but it can be controlled. However, once a dog is diagnosed with the disease, the animal will require additions of thyroid hormones for the balance of his life.

Run your hands regularly over your dog to feel for any injuries.

There is no simple answer to the question of why thyroid disease occurs with some frequency in the Akita. Heritability is certainly a factor. Most dogs appear to develop the disease at maturity, but some have symptoms while still puppies, which then progresses into severe symptoms as the dog ages.

The Orthopedic Foundation for Animals (OFA) opened a Canine Thyroid Registry to help breeders track the incidence of the disease. OFA recommends using equilibrium dialysis to test Akitas before breeding. A rating of "negative" on the certificate denotes the Akita is free of the disease when tested.

BLOAT

The Akita is at high risk for bloat, a condition that afflicts all large breeds and causes the stomach to swell up (or "bloat") from gas, food, water or a combination of all three. The dog cannot expel the gas and the stomach continues to swell until it twists (often as much as 360 degrees). This condition is called acute gastric dilation-volvulus (GDV) syndrome, or torsion. Tor-sion is a life-threatening situation. If the stomach twists, its cavity becomes sealed off, closing off the upper and lower openings through which gas may normally escape.

The swollen, distended stomach puts pressure upon internal organs, including the heart, it compresses nerves and the blood supply, and quickly results in shock and death. Immediate surgery is the only treatment for this condition. In a simple attack of bloat, in which the stomach fills with gas, the veterinarian will insert a tube down the throat, relieve the gas, pump out the stomach and give the stomach a thorough washing.

Torsion requires immediate veterinary care and surgery where the stomach is surgically "tacked down" to the body wall to prevent the twist from occurring again. Once a dog suffers from bloat, it will most likely happen again, often within days of the first attack.

Symptoms to watch for include extreme restlessness, excessive salivation, drooling, crying and an attempt to vomit or defecate. The stomach area appears swollen and the dog shows signs of pain when the abdomen is pressed. Rapid breathing, pale-colored mouth membranes and collapse are signs of shock due to a more advanced phase of bloat. If untreated, a dog will die within a short time.

SEBACEOUS ADENITIS

Sebaceous adenitis (SA) is a new disease beginning to be recognized as a serious problem in the Akita. SA is a condition in which the adult dog's sebaceous glands (oil-secreting glands that open into the hair follicles in the skin) become inflamed and are permanently destroyed. The condition is believed to be genetic, but the causes are still a mystery.

The symptoms vary but may include irreversible and progressive hair loss, thick scaly skin, chronic skin infections, a strong musky odor, and crusty skin lesions. Some Akitas develop intermittent lameness. Diagnosis requires a skin biopsy. There is no cure for this condition. Afflicted dogs should not be used in breeding until more information is available on SA. The Genodermatosis Research Foundation in Ohio, an organization dedicated to the study of inherited skin diseases in dogs, selected SA as their first project. Let us hope that we may soon have more information on this disease.

OTHER SKIN PROBLEMS

Akitas have other autoimmune diseases that cause similar skin symptoms, including **Vogt-Koyanagi-Harada (VKH) syndrome,** an autoimmune disease being seen with increasing frequency in Akitas. Affected dogs often begin to show symptoms at eighteen months to two years of age. Symptoms of VKH syndrome include loss of vision and loss of pigment with red patches on the skin, progressing to hair loss. Early diagnosis is important to prevent permanent blindness and attain any degree of success in treatment of VKH. Tests for a diagnosis include chemical analysis of the blood serum and skin biopsies.

Phemphigus foliaceus (PF) is an autoimmune skin disease seen more often in the Akita than in any other breed. It occurs when an Akita's immune system begins manufacturing antibodies against the dog's own skin, attempting to reject the skin as if it were a foreign material. The antibodies attack the skin, causing small red spots that rapidly become blisters, then pustules, and

> ### WHEN TO CALL THE VET
>
> In any emergency situation, you should call your veterinarian immediately. You can make the difference in your dog's life by staying as calm as possible when you call and by giving the doctor or the assistant as much information as possible before you leave for the clinic. That way, the vet will be able to take immediate, specific action to remedy your dog's situation.
>
> Emergencies include acute abdominal pain, suspected poisoning, snakebite, burns, frostbite, shock, dehydration, abnormal vomiting or bleeding, and deep wounds. You are the best judge of your dog's health, as you live with and observe him every day. Don't hesitate to call your veterinarian if you suspect trouble.

*An Elizabethan
collar keeps
your dog from
licking a fresh
wound.*

finally form deep crusts on the nose, ears, foot pads, and around the eyes. In some cases, crusts are found over the entire body. Loss of pigment may occur. In addition to skin symptoms, the dog may at  times be lethargic and depressed, and may show lameness, stiff joints, and, in rare cases, swelling of the abdomen and/or legs. PF can affect dogs at any age, though usually it occurs in mature dogs. Both male and female Akitas can be affected. A few drugs, usually safe for healthy Akitas, can cause severe reactions in dogs diagnosed with autoimmune disorders. These include ivermectin, some anti-inflammatory drugs and a range of sulfa drugs.

PROGRESSIVE RETINAL ATROPHY

Progressive Retinal Atrophy (PRA) is an ever-increasing genetic eye disease in Akitas as well as in many other breeds. PRA refers to a degeneration of cells in the retina and can be either gradual or progressive but always ends in blindness. There is no treatment. PRA usually becomes apparent in dogs in their prime (at about five years of age).

The form of PRA found in Akitas is thought to be inherited as a simple recessive disease, which means that dogs may carry the disorder and may pass it on to puppies, without themselves showing any signs of it. Since PRA won't show up in a dog's offspring until later in life, a dog that is a carrier may be used frequently for breeding before it has been identified as a carrier. By the time the older dog loses vision, it may have already produced a great number of puppies, thus perpetuating the problem.

Breeders are now using a new ophthalmology examination offered by the Canine Eye Registration

Foundation (CERF). A CERF number signifies that a dog's eyes are "Certified Clear of PRA" at the time of examination; however, the disease can begin to develop after the examination. Also, a CERF number does *not* mean the dog is not a carrier of PRA; it simply means the dog is not at the time of the exam afflicted with the disease or with symptoms of PRA. An early symptom of PRA is night blindness.

OTHER EYE PROBLEMS

Other eye diseases of concern in the Akita are microphthalmia and entropion. **Entropion** is a condition where an eyelid rolls inward, allowing the lashes to scratch across the cornea. This continuous abrasion results in pain, damage to the cornea and periodic infection. Untreated, it can ultimately cause blindness. Most cases of entropion involve the lower lid, though a few affect the upper lid. Runny eyes can indicate the presence of entropion. Though entropion is usually easily corrected through a simple surgical procedure, it is hereditary, so afflicted dogs should not be bred.

Microphthalmia (small eye syndrome) occurs in the Akita as well as in other breeds. This abnormally small eye can be detected in puppies as young as three weeks. Affected puppies will have cloudy small eyes, and appear to lack normal visual activity. The puppies will be unresponsive to light, they will hold their heads low and their movements will be slow and cautious. In Akitas, microphthalmia is often accompanied by cataracts (clouded lenses).

Microphthalmia is an inherited recessive trait. Normal-eyed puppies in the litter and parents of affected pups have a 60 percent chance of being a carrier of the microphthalmia gene and should not be used for breeding.

EPILEPSY

Epilepsy is an electrical disorder of the brain causing seizures of varying degrees. The seizures may be preceded by behavior changes, restlessness and anxiety. A dog having a seizure may collapse, lose consciousness for several minutes and show foaming at the mouth and head shaking. There are many types of seizures, and even more causes for them.

Seizures may be an early neurologic sign of autoimmune thyroid disease, and your veterinarian may recommend a thyroid screening to assist in determining the cause of repeated seizures. Seizures can also be caused by such diverse things as an allergic reaction to an insect bite, heatstroke, low blood sugar, liver disease, some infectious diseases (such as distemper) or brain tumors, or they can be a symptom of poisoning from many toxic materials. For this reason, your accurate observation of a triggering event is important for proper diagnosis.

If a seizure occurs, get immediate veterinary care for your Akita. Seizures can often be controlled or prevented by treating the underlying cause. If a head injury has caused brain damage that is producing the seizures, anticonvulsive drugs such may help, but they can have a toxic effect on the liver, the severity of which varies from dog to dog.

HIP DYSPLASIA (HD)

Hip dysplasia is a malformation of the hip joint which causes pain and lameness. There are varying degrees of deformity in the joint and hip X rays are the surest way to determine dysplasia. The condition causes inflammation and painful arthritis in later life. Elbow dysplasia exists in all dogs but it is not a significant problem in the Akita.

The Orthopedic Foundation for Animals (OFA) in Columbia, Missouri, offers a registry for dysplasia of hips and elbows. When a dog is two years old or older (no dog under the age of two years can receive a number), the animal's hips and elbows are X-rayed and the film is sent to the foundation. The X rays are evaluated by three radiology experts who study the hip and elbow formations. If the animal has hips and elbows that are normal for the breed, an OFA number will be assigned to the dog. If the animal shows signs of dysplasia, the foundation will not certify him to be free of the disease and he will not receive a number. Keep these facts in mind when purchasing a puppy. You want a puppy from parents certified free of dysplasia with the documentation to prove it.

OTHER CONDITIONS

The Orthopedic Foundation for Animals offers a registry to diagnose **luxating patellas,** which is a dislocation of the knee. It is an inherited problem that occurs in Akitas, usually before the dog celebrates his first birthday. It requires corrective surgery.

Tranquilizers and anesthetics are commonly used drugs to which Akitas exhibit particular sensitivity. However, the majority of veterinarians are now aware of the Akita's **sensitivity to drugs.** Discuss this with your own vet before allowing your Akita to undergo any surgical procedure or to use any tranquilizing drugs.

The Akita has been found to have red blood cells with a **high potassium** content. All other canines have red cells with a low potassium content. This high potassium content has not been linked to any disease, but it can cause a problem during routine blood panels if your veterinarian is not familiar with this curiosity. If the blood is not stored properly, the potassium leaks from the red cells into the plasma and gives a false indication of Addison's disease syndrome. (Addison's disease is the failure of the adrenal glands.) Little is understood about this high potassium level in the Akita, but the information can save you a good scare if your veterinarian is unfamiliar with the breed.

The Aging Akita

Good food, exercise and love will keep the Akita thriving for ten to fourteen years.

An annual routine health check-up, including laboratory health profiling, is a good way to identify problems early and institute corrective or treatment measures.

WEIGHT AND EXERCISE

As a dog ages, his activity levels naturally slow down. If you continue feeding the same amount of food with the same fat and calorie content, the decrease of activity will eventually result in obesity. This condition shortens the dog's life. A gain of 10 percent is considered critical. A fat dog is at risk from heart disease, increased surgical and anesthetic risk, pancreatitis, intestinal gas, diabetes and other metabolic problems, as well as bone and joint diseases.

How can you tell if your Akita is obese? Run the flat of your hand along your dog's rib cage and the underside of his trunk. If you can feel the ribs, your Akita is at a good weight. If you can feel pads of fat, please refer to chapter 5 for weight control.

Regular, moderate exercise is still necessary at this mature stage of your Akita's life. Do not allow your Akita to sleep away the rest of his life; keep him active with daily walks and continue to encourage regular play periods.

ARTHRITIS

When an older dog develops stiffness in the rear legs, it is usually a sign of arthritis, a disease that occurs in nearly all aging creatures, including humans. If your animal is suffering from arthritis you may wish to try some of the following supplements which are helpful when given regularly. Yucca acts as a natural anti-inflammatory and helps relieve symptoms of arthritis—three tablets twice daily for a large dog is recommended.

Perhaps the most effective arthritis relief is glucosamine sulfate, an amino-monosaccharide present in the body as a component of cartilage. Apparently it stimulates production of synovial fluid, which is present in all joints as a cushion and assists in healing damaged cartilage. Some animals may not efficiently convert glucosamine sulfate into its more usable form as N-acetylglucosamine (NAG); therefore, a combination of both is recommended. The usual dosage is 500 milligrams three times a day. Patience and diligence are required with this treatment since improvement may not begin until the fourth week, but when the supplement takes effect, progress is amazing.

CANCER

Early diagnosis of a potential cancer is important. Frequently examine your female Akita's mammary glands. While the dog is lying on her back, check each nipple for any enlargement or deformity. Gently feel around each nipple for any lumps. If you find any abnormalities, she should be checked by your veterinarian immediately, as malignancy often progresses rapidly.

Male Akitas can develop prostate gland problems, ranging from constipation caused by the enlargement of the prostate gland to infections and cancer of the gland. Signs to watch for include difficult or painful defecation, difficult or painful urination and blood in the urine. Loss of appetite and pain in the pelvic area also can signal a prostate problem. This condition requires immediate veterinary attention.

HEART AND KIDNEY DISEASE

Akitas do not often suffer from heart disease, but you should be aware of the basic symptoms. Continuous heavy panting during exertion, difficulty in breathing, a deep cough, listlessness or bluish colored gums or tongue can all suggest heart problems and require immediate veterinary care.

One major cause of death in old Akitas is kidney failure. The kidneys filter the blood under pressure, and then reabsorb water and selected substances back into the blood. During this process waste products are deposited in the urine and excreted from the body. Older dogs often suffer from decreased kidney function and may require a special diet. This loss of kidney function is irreversible, but it is not usually fatal unless allowed to progress without treatment.

Saying Good-bye

If you decide your older Akita is no longer enjoying life, is incontinent, severely crippled or disease-ridden and in constant pain, euthanasia is the humane alternative to a degrading existence. Dignity is very important to an Akita of any age. In this regard, humanely ending your Akita's life is the ultimate consideration you can give the dog that gave you years of love and companionship. Take him to your regular veterinarian, a person he knows, and remain with him while he is given an injection of euthanol fluid. His death will be free from feelings of fear and rejection.

The process of euthanasia is painless and quick for the dog but to your children and family members it can be traumatic. Your veterinarian can give you information on local grief support groups to help you through this difficult time.

Your Happy, Healthy Pet

Your Dog's Name _____

Name on Your Dog's Pedigree (if your dog has one) _____

_____

Where Your Dog Came From _____

_____

Your Dog's Birthday _____

Your Dog's Veterinarian

    Name _____

    Address _____

    Phone Number_____

    Emergency Number_____

Your Dog's Health

    Vaccines

        type _____ date given _____

        type _____ date given _____

        type _____ date given _____

        type _____ date given _____

    Heartworm

        date tested _____ type used_____ start date _____

Your Dog's License Number_____

Groomer's Name and Number _____

Dogsitter/Walker's Name and Number_____

Awards Your Dog Has Won

    Award _____ date earned _____

    Award _____ date earned _____

part three

Enjoying
your
Dog

chapter 8

Basic
Training

by Ian Dunbar, Ph.D., MRCVS

Training is the jewel in the crown—the most important aspect of doggy husbandry. There is no more important variable influencing dog behavior and temperament than the dog's education: A well-trained, well-behaved and good-natured puppydog is always a joy to live with, but an untrained and uncivilized dog can be a perpetual nightmare. Moreover, deny the dog an education and it will not have the opportunity to fulfill its own canine potential; neither will it have the ability to communicate effectively with its human companions.

Luckily, modern psychological training methods are easy, efficient and effective and, above all, considerably dog-friendly and user-friendly. Doggy education is as simple as it is enjoyable. But before you can have a good time play-training with your new dog, you have to learn what to do and how to do it. There is no bigger variable influencing the success of dog training than the *owner's* experience and expertise. *Before you embark on the dog's education, you must first educate yourself.*

Basic Training for Owners

Ideally, basic owner training should begin well *before* you select your dog. Find out all you can about your chosen breed first, then master rudimentary training and handling skills. If you already have your puppy/dog, owner training is a dire emergency—the clock is running! Especially for puppies, the first few weeks at home are the most important and influential days in the dog's life. Indeed, the cause of most adolescent and adult problems may be traced back to the initial days the pup explores his new home. This is the time to establish the *status quo*—to teach the puppy/dog how you would like him to behave and so prevent otherwise quite predictable problems.

In addition to consulting breeders and breed books such as this one (which understandably have a positive breed bias), seek out as many pet owners with your breed you can find. Good points are obvious. What you want to find out are the breed-specific *problems*, so you can nip them in the bud. In particular, you should talk to owners with *adolescent* dogs and make a list of all anticipated problems. Most important, *test drive* at least half a dozen adolescent and adult dogs of your breed yourself. An eight-week-old puppy is deceptively easy to handle, but she will acquire adult size, speed and strength in just four months, so you should learn now what to prepare for.

Puppy and pet dog training classes offer a convenient venue to locate pet owners and observe dogs in action. For a list of suitable trainers in your area, contact the Association of Pet Dog Trainers (see Chapter 13). You may also begin your basic owner training by observing other owners in class. Watch as many classes and test drive as many dogs as possible. Select an upbeat, dog-friendly, people-friendly, fun-and-games, puppydog pet training class to learn the ropes. Also, watch training videos and read training books (see Chapter 12). You must find out what to do and how to do it *before* you have to do it.

Principles of Training

Most people think training comprises teaching the dog to do things such as sit, speak and roll over, but even a four-week-old pup knows how to do these things already. Instead, the first step in training involves teaching the dog human words for each dog behavior and activity and for each aspect of the dog's environment. That way you, the owner, can more easily participate in the dog's domestic education by directing him to perform specific actions appropriately, that is, at the right time, in the right place, and so on. Training opens communication channels, enabling an educated dog to at least understand the owner's requests.

In addition to teaching a dog *what* we want her to do, it is also necessary to teach her *why* she should do what we ask. Indeed, 95 percent of training revolves around motivating the dog *to want to do* what we want. Dogs often understand what their owners want; they just don't see the point of doing it—especially when the owner's repetitively boring and seemingly senseless instructions are totally at odds with much more pressing and exciting doggy distractions. It is not so much the dog who is being stubborn or dominant; rather, it is the owner who has failed to acknowledge the dog's needs and feelings and to approach training from the dog's point of view.

The Meaning of Instructions

The secret to successful training is learning how to use training lures to predict or prompt specific behaviors—to coax the dog to do what you want *when* you want. Any highly valued object (such as a treat or toy) may be used as a lure, which the dog will follow with his eyes and nose. Moving the lure in specific ways entices the dog to move his nose, head and entire body in specific ways. In fact, by learning the art of manipulating various lures, it is possible to teach the dog to assume virtually any body position and perform any action. Once you have control over the expression of the dog's behaviors and can elicit any body position or behavior at will, you can easily teach the dog to perform on request.

Tell your dog what you want him to do, use a lure to entice him to respond correctly, then profusely praise

Teach your dog words for each activity he needs to know, like down.

and maybe reward him once he performs the desired action. For example, verbally request "Fido, sit!" while you move a squeaky toy upwards and backwards over the dog's muzzle (lure-movement and hand signal), smile knowingly as he looks up (to follow the lure) and sits down (as a result of canine anatomical engineering), then praise him to distraction ("Gooood Fido!"). Squeak the toy, offer a training treat and give your dog and yourself a pat on the back.

Being able to elicit desired responses over and over enables the owner to reward the dog over and over. Consequently, the dog begins to think training is fun. For example, the more the dog is rewarded for sitting, the more she enjoys sitting. Eventually the dog comes to realize that, whereas most sitting is appreciated, sitting immediately upon request usually prompts especially enthusiastic praise and a slew of high-level rewards. The dog begins to sit on cue much of the time, showing that she is starting to grasp the meaning of the owner's verbal request and hand signal.

Why Comply?

Most dogs enjoy initial lure/reward training and are only too happy to comply with their owners' wishes. Unfortunately, repetitive drilling without appreciative feedback tends to diminish the dog's enthusiasm until he eventually fails to see the point of complying anymore. Moreover, as the dog approaches adolescence he becomes more easily distracted as he develops other interests. Lengthy sessions with repetitive exercises tend to bore and demotivate both parties. If it's not fun, the owner doesn't do it and neither does the dog.

Integrate training into your dog's life: The greater number of training sessions each day and the *shorter* they are, the more willingly compliant your dog will become. Make sure to have a short (just a few seconds) training interlude before every enjoyable canine activity. For example, ask your dog to sit to greet people, to sit before you throw his Frisbee, and to sit for his supper. Really, sitting is no different from a canine "please." Also, include numerous short training interludes during every enjoyable canine pastime, for example, when playing with the dog or when he is running in the park. In this fashion, doggy distractions may be effectively converted into rewards for training. Just as all games have rules, fun becomes training . . . and training becomes fun.

Eventually, rewards actually become unnecessary to continue motivating your dog. If trained with consideration and kindness, performing the desired behaviors will become self-rewarding and, in a sense, your dog will motivate himself. Just as it is not necessary to reward a human companion during an enjoyable walk in the park, or following a game of tennis, it is hardly necessary to reward our best friend—the dog—for walking by our side or while playing fetch. Human company during enjoyable activities is reward enough for most dogs.

Even though your dog has become self-motivating, it's still good to praise and pet him a lot and offer rewards once in a while, especially for a good job well done. And if for no other reason, praising and rewarding others is good for the human heart.

To train your dog, you need gentle hands, a loving heart and a good attitude.

Punishment

Without a doubt, lure/reward training is by far the best way to teach: Entice your dog to do what you want and then reward him for doing so. Unfortunately, a human shortcoming is to take the good for granted and to moan and groan at the bad. Specifically, the dog's many good behaviors are ignored while the owner focuses on punishing the dog for making mistakes. In extreme cases, instruction is *limited* to punishing mistakes made by a trainee dog, child, employee or husband, even though it has been proven punishment training is notoriously inefficient and ineffective and is decidedly unfriendly and combative. It teaches the dog that training is a drag, almost as quickly as it teaches the dog to dislike his trainer. Why treat our best friends like our worst enemies?

Punishment training is also much more laborious and time consuming. Whereas it takes only a finite amount of time to teach a dog what to chew, for example, it takes much, much longer to punish the dog for each and every mistake. Remember, *there is only one right way!* So why not teach that right way from the outset?!

To make matters worse, punishment training causes severe lapses in the dog's reliability. Since it is obviously impossible to punish the dog each and every time she misbehaves, the dog quickly learns to distinguish between those times when she must comply (so as to avoid impending punishment) and those times when she need not comply, because punishment is impossible. Such times include when the dog is off leash and only six feet away, when the owner is otherwise engaged (talking to a friend, watching television, taking a shower, tending to the baby or chatting on the telephone), or when the dog is left at home alone.

Instances of misbehavior will be numerous when the owner is away, because even when the dog complied in the owner's looming presence, he did so unwillingly. The dog was forced to act against his will, rather than moulding his will to want to please. Hence, when the owner is absent, not only does the dog know he need not comply, he simply does not want to. Again, the trainee is not a stubborn vindictive beast, but rather the trainer has failed to teach.

Punishment training invariably creates unpredictable Jekyll and Hyde behavior.

Trainer's Tools

Many training books extol the virtues of a vast array of training paraphernalia and electronic and metallic gizmos, most of which are designed for canine restraint, correction and punishment, rather than for actual facilitation of doggy education. In reality, most effective training tools are not found in stores; they come from within ourselves. In addition to a willing dog, all you really need is a functional human brain, gentle hands, a loving heart and a good attitude.

In terms of equipment, all dogs do require a quality buckle collar to sport dog tags and to attach the leash (for safety and to comply with local leash laws). Hollow chewtoys (like Kongs or sterilized longbones) and a dog bed or collapsible crate are a must for housetraining. Three additional tools are required:

1. specific lures (training treats and toys) to predict and prompt specific desired behaviors;

2. rewards (praise, affection, training treats and toys) to reinforce for the dog what a lot of fun it all is; and

3. knowledge—how to convert the dog's favorite activities and games (potential distractions to training) into "life-rewards," which may be employed to facilitate training.

The most powerful of these is *knowledge*. Education is the key! Watch training classes, participate in training classes, watch videos, read books, enjoy playtraining with your dog, and then your dog will say "Please," and your dog will say "Thank you!"

Housetraining

If dogs were left to their own devices, certainly they would chew, dig and bark for entertainment and then no doubt highlight a few areas of their living space with sprinkles of urine, in much the same way we decorate by hanging pictures. Consequently, when we ask a dog to live with us, we must teach him *where* he may dig and perform his toilet duties, *what* he may chew and *when* he may bark. After all, when left at home alone for many hours, we cannot expect the dog to amuse himself by completing crosswords or watching the soaps on TV!

Also, it would be decidedly unfair to keep the house rules a secret from the dog, and then get angry and punish the poor critter for inevitably transgressing rules he did not even know existed. Remember, without adequate education and guidance, the dog will be forced to establish his own rules—doggy rules—that most probably will be at odds with the owner's view of domestic living.

Since most problems develop during the first few days the dog is at home, prospective dog owners must be certain they are quite clear about the principles of housetraining *before* they get a dog. Early misbehaviors quickly become established as the status quo—

becoming firmly entrenched as hard-to-break bad habits, which set the precedent for years to come. Make sure to teach your dog good habits right from the start. Good habits are just as hard to break as bad ones!

Ideally, when a new dog comes home, try to arrange for someone to be present for as much as possible during the first few days (for adult dogs) or weeks for puppies. With only a little forethought, it is surprisingly easy to find a puppy sitter, such as a retired person, who would be willing to eat from your refrigerator and watch your television while keeping an eye on the newcomer to encourage the dog to play with chewtoys and to ensure he goes outside on a regular basis.

POTTY TRAINING

To teach the dog where to relieve himself:

1. never let him make a single mistake;
2. let him know where you want him to go; and
3. handsomely reward him for doing so: "GOOOOOOOD DOG!!!" liver treat, liver treat, liver treat!

PREVENTING MISTAKES

A single mistake is a training disaster, since it heralds many more in future weeks. And each time the dog soils the house, this further reinforces the dog's unfortunate preference for an indoor, carpeted toilet. *Do not let an unhousetrained dog have full run of the house if you are away from home or cannot pay full attention.* Instead, confine the dog to an area where elimination is appropriate, such as an outdoor run or, better still, a small, comfortable indoor kennel with access to an outdoor run. When confined in this manner, most dogs will naturally housetrain themselves.

If that's not possible, confine the dog to an area, such as a utility room, kitchen, basement or garage, where elimination may not be desired in the long run but as an interim measure it is certainly preferable to doing it all around the house. Use newspaper to cover the floor of the dog's day room. The newspaper may be used to soak up the urine and to wrap up and dispose of the feces. Once your dog develops a preferred spot for eliminating, it is only necessary to cover that part of the floor with newspaper. The smaller papered area may then be moved (only a little each day) towards the door to the outside. Thus the dog will develop the tendency to go to the door when he needs to relieve himself.

Never confine an unhousetrained dog to a crate for long periods. Doing so would force the dog to soil the crate and ruin its usefulness as an aid for housetraining (see the following discussion).

The first few weeks at home are the most important and influential in your dog's life

TEACHING WHERE

In order to teach your dog where you would like her to do her business, you have to be there to direct the proceedings—an obvious, yet often neglected, fact of life. In order to be there to teach the dog *where* to go, you need to know *when* she needs to go. Indeed, the success of housetraining depends on the owner's ability to predict these times. Certainly, a regular feeding schedule will facilitate prediction somewhat, but there is nothing like "loading the deck" and influencing the timing of the outcome yourself!

Whenever you are at home, make sure the dog is under constant supervision and/or confined to a small area. If already well trained, simply instruct the dog to lie down in his bed or basket. Alternatively, confine the dog to a crate (doggy den) or tie-down (a short, 18-inch lead that can be clipped to an eye hook in the baseboard). Short-term close confinement strongly inhibits urination and defecation, since the dog does not want to soil his sleeping area. Thus, when you release the puppydog each hour, he will definitely need to urinate immediately and defecate every third or fourth hour. Keep the dog confined to his doggy den and take him to his intended toilet area each hour, every hour, and on the hour.

When taking your dog outside, instruct him to sit quietly before opening the door—he will soon learn to sit by the door when he needs to go out!

TEACHING WHY

Being able to predict when the dog needs to go enables the owner to be on the spot to praise and reward the dog. Each hour, hurry the dog to the intended toilet area in the yard, issue the appropriate instruction ("Go pee!" or "Go poop!"), then give the dog three to four minutes to produce. Praise and offer a couple of training treats when successful. The treats are important because many people fail to praise their dogs with feeling . . . and housetraining is hardly the time for understatement. So either loosen up and enthusiastically praise that dog: "Wuzzzer-wuzzer-wuzzer, hoooser good wuffer den? Hoooo went pee for Daddy?" Or say "Good dog!" as best you can and offer the treats for effect.

Following elimination is an ideal time for a spot of playtraining in the yard or house. Also, an empty dog may be allowed greater freedom around the house for the next half hour or so, just as long as you keep an eye out to make sure he does not get into other kinds of mischief. If you are preoccupied and cannot pay full attention, confine the dog to his doggy den once more to enjoy a peaceful snooze or to play with his many chewtoys.

If your dog does not eliminate within the allotted time outside—no biggie! Back to his doggy den, and then try again after another hour.

As I own large dogs, I always feel more relaxed walking an empty dog, knowing that I will not need to finish our stroll weighted down with bags of feces! Beware of falling into the trap of walking the dog to get it to eliminate. The good ol' dog walk is such an enormous highlight in the dog's life that it represents the single biggest potential reward in domestic dogdom. However, when in a hurry, or during inclement weather, many owners abruptly terminate the walk the moment the dog has done its business. This, in effect, severely punishes the dog for doing the right thing, in the right place at the right time. Consequently, many dogs become strongly inhibited from eliminating outdoors because they know it will signal an abrupt end to an otherwise thoroughly enjoyable walk.

Instead, instruct the dog to relieve himself in the yard prior to going for a walk. If you follow the above instructions, most dogs soon learn to eliminate on cue. As soon as the dog eliminates, praise (and offer a treat or two)—"Good dog! Let's go walkies!" Use the walk as a reward for eliminating in the yard. If the dog does not go, put him back in his doggy den and think about a walk later on. You will find with a "No feces–no walk" policy, your dog will become one of the fastest defecators in the business.

If you do not have a back yard, instruct the dog to eliminate right outside your front door prior to the walk. Not only will this facilitate clean up and disposal of the feces in your own trash can but, also, the walk may again be used as a colossal reward.

CHEWING AND BARKING

Short-term close confinement also teaches the dog that occasional quiet moments are a reality of domestic living. Your puppydog is extremely impressionable during his first few weeks at home. Regular

confinement at this time soon exerts a calming influ-
ence over the dog's personality. Remember, once the
dog is housetrained and calmer, there will be a whole
lifetime ahead for the dog to enjoy full run of the
house and garden. On the other hand, by letting the
newcomer have unrestricted access to the entire household and allowing him to run willy-nilly, he will most
certainly develop a bunch of behavior problems in
short order, no doubt necessitating confinement later
in life. It would not be fair to remedially restrain and
confine a dog you have trained, through neglect, to
run free.

When confining the dog, make sure he always has an
impressive array of suitable chewtoys. Kongs and sterilized longbones (both readily available from pet stores)
make the best chewtoys, since they are hollow and may
be stuffed with treats to heighten the dog's interest.
For example, by stuffing the little hole at the top of a
Kong with a small piece of freeze-dried liver, the dog
will not want to leave it alone.

Remember, treats do not have to be junk food and they
certainly should not represent extra calories. Rather,
treats should be part of each dog's regular daily diet:

*Make sure your
puppy has suit-
able chewtoys.*

Some food may be
served in the dog's
bowl for breakfast and
dinner, some food
may be used as train-
ing treats, and some
food may be used for
stuffing chewtoys. I
regularly stuff my
dogs' many Kongs
with different shaped
biscuits and kibble.
The kibble seems to fall out fairly easily, as do the
oval-shaped biscuits, thus rewarding the dog instanta-
neously for checking out the chewtoys. The bone-
shaped biscuits fall out after a while, rewarding the dog
for worrying at the chewtoy. But the triangular biscuits
never come out. They remain inside the Kong as lures,

maintaining the dog's fascination with its chewtoy. To further focus the dog's interest, I always make sure to flavor the triangular biscuits by rubbing them with a little cheese or freeze-dried liver.

If stuffed chewtoys are reserved especially for times the dog is confined, the puppy-dog will soon learn to enjoy quiet moments in her doggy den and she will quickly develop a chewtoy habit—a good habit! This is a simple *passive training* process; all the owner has to do is set up the situation and the dog all but trains herself—easy and effective. Even when the dog is given run of the house, her first inclination will be to indulge her rewarding chewtoy habit rather than destroying less-attractive household articles, such as curtains, carpets, chairs and compact disks. Similarly, a chewtoy chewer will be less inclined to scratch and chew herself excessively. Also, if the dog busies herself as a recreational chewer, she will be less inclined to develop into a recreational barker or digger when left at home alone.

Stuff a number of chewtoys whenever the dog is left confined and remove the extra-special-tasting treats when you return. Your dog will now amuse himself with his chewtoys before falling asleep and then resume playing with his chewtoys when he expects you to return. Since most owner-absent misbehavior happens right after you leave and right before your expected return, your puppydog will now be conveniently preoccupied with his chewtoys at these times.

Come and Sit

Most puppies will happily approach virtually anyone, whether called or not; that is, until they collide with

To teach come, call your dog, open your arms as a welcoming signal, wave a toy or a treat and praise for every step in your direction.

adolescence and develop other more important doggy interests, such as sniffing a multiplicity of exquisite odors on the grass. Your mission, Mr. and/or Ms. Owner, is to teach and reward the pup for coming reliably, willingly and happily when called—and you have just three months to get it done. Unless adequately reinforced, your puppy's tendency to approach people will self-destruct by adolescence.

Call your dog ("Fido, come!"), open your arms (and maybe squat down) as a welcoming signal, waggle a treat or toy as a lure, and reward the puppydog when he comes running. Do not wait to praise the dog until he reaches you—he may come 95 percent of the way and then run off after some distraction. Instead, praise the dog's *first* step towards you and continue praising enthusiastically for *every* step he takes in your direction.

When the rapidly approaching puppy dog is three lengths away from impact, instruct him to sit ("Fido, sit!") and hold the lure in front of you in an outstretched hand to prevent him from hitting you midchest and knocking you flat on your back! As Fido decelerates to nose the lure, move the treat upwards and backwards just over his muzzle with an upwards motion of your extended arm (palm-upwards). As the dog looks up to follow the lure, he will sit down (if he jumps up, you are holding the lure too high). Praise the dog for sitting. Move backwards and call him again. Repeat this many times over, always praising when Fido comes and sits; on occasion, reward him.

For the first couple of trials, use a training treat both as a lure to entice the dog to come and sit and as a reward for doing so. Thereafter, try to use different items as lures and rewards. For example, lure the dog with a Kong or Frisbee but reward her with a food treat. Or lure the dog with a food treat but pat her and throw a tennis ball as a reward. After just a few repetitions, dispense with the lures and rewards; the dog will begin to respond willingly to your verbal requests and hand signals just for the prospect of praise from your heart and affection from your hands.

Instruct every family member, friend and visitor how to get the dog to come and sit. Invite people over for a series of pooch parties; do not keep the pup a secret—let other people enjoy this puppy, and let the pup enjoy other people. Puppydog parties are not only fun, they easily attract a lot of people to help *you* train *your* dog. Unless you teach your dog *how* to meet people, that is, to sit for greetings, no doubt the dog will resort to jumping up. Then you and the visitors will get annoyed, and the dog will be punished. This is not fair. *Send out those invitations for puppy parties and teach your dog to be mannerly and socially acceptable.*

Even though your dog quickly masters obedient recalls in the house, his reliability may falter when playing in the back yard or local park. Ironically, it is *the owner* who has unintentionally trained the dog *not* to respond in these instances. By allowing the dog to play and run around and otherwise have a good time, but then to call the dog to put him on leash to take him home, the dog quickly learns playing is fun but training is a drag. Thus, playing in the park becomes a severe distraction, which works against training. Bad news!

Instead, whether playing with the dog off leash or on leash, request him to come at frequent intervals—say, every minute or so. On most occasions, praise and pet the dog for a few seconds while he is sitting, then tell him to go play again. For especially fast recalls, offer a couple of training treats and take the time to praise and pet the dog enthusiastically before releasing him. The dog will learn that coming when called is not necessarily the end of the play session, and neither is it the end of the world; rather, it signals an enjoyable, quality time-out with the owner before resuming play once more. In fact, playing in the park now becomes a very effective life-reward, which works to facilitate training by reinforcing each obedient and timely recall. Good news!

Sit, Down, Stand and Rollover

Teaching the dog a variety of body positions is easy for owner and dog, impressive for spectators and extremely useful for all. Using lure-reward techniques, it is possible to train several positions at once to verbal commands or hand signals (which impress the socks off onlookers).

Sit and *down*—the two control commands—prevent or resolve nearly a hundred behavior problems. For example, if the dog happily and obediently sits or lies down when requested, he cannot jump on visitors, dash out the front door, run around and chase its tail, pester other dogs, harass cats or annoy family, friends or strangers. Additionally, "sit" or "down" are better emergency commands for off-leash control.

It is easier to teach and maintain a reliable sit than maintain a reliable recall. *Sit* is the purest and simplest of commands—either the dog is sitting or he is not. If there is any change of circumstances or potential danger in the park, for example, simply instruct the dog to sit. If he sits, you have a number of options: allow the dog to resume playing when he is safe; walk up and put the dog on leash, or call the dog. The dog will be much more likely to come when called if he has already acknowledged his compliance by sitting. If the dog does not sit in the park—train him to!

Stand and *rollover-stay* are the two positions for examining the dog. Your veterinarian will love you to distraction if you take a little time to teach the dog to stand still and roll over and play possum. Also, your vet bills will be smaller. The rollover-stay is an especially useful command and is really just a variation of the down-stay: whereas the dog lies prone in the traditional down, she lies supine in the rollover-stay.

As with teaching come and sit, the training techniques to teach the dog to assume all other body positions on cue are user-friendly and dog-friendly. Simply give the appropriate request, lure the dog into the desired body position using a training treat or toy and then *praise* (and maybe reward) the dog as soon as he complies. Try not to touch the dog to get him to respond. If you teach the dog by guiding him into position, the dog will quickly learn that rump-pressure means sit, for example, but as yet you still have no control over your dog if he is just six feet away. It will still be necessary to teach the dog to sit on request. So do not make training a time-consuming two-step process; instead, teach the dog to sit to a verbal request or hand signal from the outset. Once the dog sits willingly when requested, by all means use your hands to pet the dog when he does so.

To teach *down* when the dog is already sitting, say "Fido, down!," hold the lure in one hand (palm down) and lower that hand to the floor between the dog's forepaws. As the dog lowers his head to follow the lure, slowly move the lure away from the dog just a fraction (in front of his paws). The dog will lie down as he stretches his nose forward to follow the lure. Praise the dog when he does so. If the dog stands up, you pulled the lure away too far and too quickly.

When teaching the dog to lie down from the standing position, say "down" and lower the lure to the floor as before. Once the dog has lowered his forequarters and assumed a play bow, gently and slowly move the lure *towards* the dog between his forelegs. Praise the dog as soon as his rear end plops down.

After just a couple of trials it will be possible to alternate sits and downs and have the dog energetically perform doggy push-ups. Praise the dog a lot, and after half a dozen or so push-ups reward the dog with a training treat or toy. You will notice the more energetically you move your arm—upwards (palm up) to get the dog to sit, and downwards (palm down) to get the dog to lie down—the more energetically the dog responds to your requests. Now try training the dog in silence and you will notice he has also learned to respond to hand signals. Yeah! Not too shabby for the first session.

To teach *stand* from the sitting position, say "Fido, stand," slowly move the lure half a dog-length away from the dog's nose, keeping it at nose level, and praise the dog as he stands to follow the lure. As soon

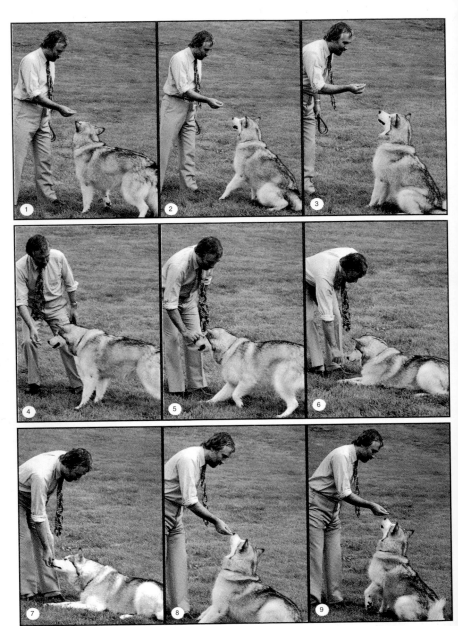

Using a food lure to teach sit, down and stand. 1) "Phoenix, Sit." 2) Hand palm upwards, move lure up and back over dog's muzzle. 3) "Good sit, Phoenix!" 4) "Phoenix, down." 5) Hand palm downwards, move lure down to lie between dog's forepaws. 6) "Phoenix, off. Good down, Phoenix!" 7) "Phoenix, sit!" 8) Palm upwards, move lure up and back, keeping it close to dog's muzzle. 9) "Good sit, Phoenix!"

10) "Phoenix, stand!" 11) Move lure away from dog at nose height, then lower it a tad. 12) "Phoenix, off! Good stand, Phoenix!" 13) "Phoenix, down!" 14) Hand palm downwards, move lure down to lie between dog's forepaws. 15) "Phoenix, off! Good down-stay, Phoenix!" 16) "Phoenix, stand!" 17) Move lure away from dog's muzzle up to nose height. 18) "Phoenix, off! Good stand-stay, Phoenix. Now we'll make the vet and groomer happy!"

as the dog stands, lower the lure to just beneath the dog's chin to entice him to look down; otherwise he will stand and then sit immediately. To prompt the dog to stand from the down position, move the lure half a dog-length upwards and away from the dog, holding the lure at standing nose height from the floor.

Teaching *rollover* is best started from the down position, with the dog lying on one side, or at least with both hind legs stretched out on the same side. Say "Fido, bang!" and move the lure backwards and alongside the dog's muzzle to its elbow (on the side of its outstretched hind legs). Once the dog looks to the side and backwards, very slowly move the lure upwards to the dog's shoulder and backbone. Tickling the dog in the goolies (groin area) often invokes a reflex-raising of the hind leg as an appeasement gesture, which facilitates the tendency to roll over. If you move the lure too quickly and the dog jumps into the standing position, have patience and start again. As soon as the dog rolls onto its back, keep the lure stationary and mesmerize the dog with a relaxing tummy rub.

To teach *rollover-stay* when the dog is standing or moving, say "Fido, bang!" and give the appropriate hand signal (with index finger pointed and thumb cocked in true Sam Spade fashion), then in one fluid movement lure him to first lie down and then rollover-stay as above.

Teaching the dog to *stay* in each of the above four positions becomes a piece of cake after first teaching the dog not to worry at the toy or treat training lure. This is best accomplished by hand feeding dinner kibble. Hold a piece of kibble firmly in your hand and softly instruct "Off!" Ignore any licking and slobbering *for however long the dog worries at the treat*, but say "Take it!" and offer the kibble *the instant* the dog breaks contact with his muzzle. Repeat this a few times, and then up the ante and insist the dog remove his muzzle for one whole second before offering the kibble. Then progressively refine your criteria and have the dog not touch your hand (or treat) for longer and longer periods on each trial, such as for two seconds, four seconds, then six, ten, fifteen, twenty, thirty seconds and so on. The dog soon learns: (1) worrying at the treat never gets results, whereas (2) noncontact is often rewarded after a variable time lapse.

Teaching *"Off!"* has many useful applications in its own right. Additionally, instructing the dog not to touch a training lure often produces spontaneous and magical stays. Request the dog to stand-stay, for example, and not to touch the lure. At first set your sights on a short two-second stay before rewarding the dog. (Remember, every long journey begins with a single step.) However, on subsequent trials, gradually and progressively increase the length of stay required to receive a reward. In no time at all your dog will stand calmly for a minute or so.

Relevancy Training

Once you have taught the dog what you expect her to do when requested to come, sit, lie down, stand, rollover and stay, the time is right to teach the dog *why* she should comply with your wishes. The secret is to have many (*many*) extremely short training interludes (two to five seconds each) at numerous (*numerous*) times during the course of the dog's day. Especially work with the dog immediately *before* the dog's good times and *during* the dog's good times. For example, ask your dog to sit and/or lie down each time before opening doors, serving meals, offering treats and tummy rubs; ask the dog to perform a few controlled doggy push-ups before letting her off-leash or throwing a tennis ball; and perhaps request the dog to sit-down-sit-stand-down-stand-rollover before inviting her to cuddle on the couch.

Similarly, request the dog to sit many times during play or on walks, and in no time at all the dog will be only too pleased to follow your instructions because he has learned that a compliant response heralds all sorts of goodies. Basically all you are trying to teach the dog is how to say please: "Please throw the tennis ball. Please may I snuggle on the couch."

Remember, whereas it is important to keep training interludes short, it is equally important to have many short sessions each and every day. The shortest (and most useful) session comprises asking the dog to sit and then go play during a play session. When trained this way, your dog will soon associate training with good times. In fact, the dog may be unable to distinguish between training and good times and, indeed, there should be no distinction. The warped concept that training involves forcing the dog to comply and/or dominating his will is totally at odds with the picture of a truly well-trained dog. In reality, enjoying a game of training with a dog is no different from enjoying a game of backgammon or tennis with a friend; and walking with a dog should be no different from strolling with buddies on the golf course.

Walk by Your Side

Many people attempt to teach a dog to heel by putting him on a leash and physically correcting the dog when he makes mistakes. There are a number of things seriously wrong with this approach, the first being that most people do not want precision heeling; rather, they simply want the dog to follow or walk by their side. Second, when physically restrained during "training," even though the dog may grudgingly mope by your side when "handcuffed" on leash, let's see what happens when he is off leash. History! The dog is in the next county because he never enjoyed walking with you on leash and you have no control over him off leash. So let's just teach the dog off leash from the outset to *want* to walk with us. Third, if the dog has not been trained to heel, it is a trifle hasty to think about punishing the poor dog for making mistakes and breaking heeling rules he didn't even know existed. This is simply not fair! Surely, if the dog had been adequately taught how to heel, he would seldom make mistakes and hence there would be no need to correct the dog. Remember, each mistake and each correction (punishment) advertise the trainer's inadequacy, not the dog's. The dog is not stubborn, he is not stupid and he is not bad. Even if he were, he would still require training, so let's train him properly.

Let's teach the dog to *enjoy* following us and to *want* to walk by our side offleash. Then it will be easier to teach high-precision off-leash heeling patterns if desired. After attaching the leash for safety on outdoor walks, but before going anywhere, it is necessary to teach the dog specifically not to pull. Now it will be much easier to teach on-leash walking and heeling because the dog already wants to walk with you, he is familiar with the desired walking and heeling positions and he knows not to pull.

FOLLOWING

Start by training your dog to follow you. Many puppies will follow if you simply walk away from them and maybe click your fingers or chuckle. Adult dogs may require additional enticement to stimulate them to follow, such as a training lure or, at the very least, a lively trainer. To teach the dog to follow: (1) keep walking and (2) walk away from the dog. If the dog attempts to lead or lag, change pace; slow down if the dog forges too far ahead, but speed up if he lags too far behind. Say "Steady!" or "Easy!" each time before you slow down and "Quickly!" or "Hustle!" each time before you speed up, and the dog will learn to change pace on cue. If the dog lags or leads too far, or if he wanders right or left, simply walk quickly in the opposite direction and maybe even run away from the dog and hide.

Practicing is a lot of fun; you can set up a course in your home, yard or park to do this. Indoors, entice the dog to follow upstairs, into a bedroom, into the bathroom, downstairs, around the living room couch, zigzagging between dining room chairs and into the kitchen for dinner. Outdoors, get the dog to follow around park benches, trees, shrubs and along walkways and lines in the grass. (For safety outdoors, it is advisable to attach a long line on the dog, but never exert corrective tension on the line.)

Enjoying Your
Dog

Remember, following has a lot to do with attitude—
your attitude! Most probably your dog will *not* want to
follow Mr. Grumpy Troll with the personality of wilted
lettuce. Lighten up—walk with a jaunty step, whistle a
happy tune, sing, skip and tell jokes to your dog and he
will be right there by your side.

BY YOUR SIDE

It is smart to train the dog to walk close on one side or
the other—either side will do, your choice. When walking, jogging or cycling, it is generally bad news to have
the dog suddenly cut in front of you. In fact, I train my
dogs to walk "By my side" and "Other side"—both very
useful instructions. It is possible to position the dog
fairly accurately by looking to the appropriate side and
clicking your fingers or slapping your thigh on that
side. A precise positioning may be attained by holding
a training lure, such as a chewtoy, tennis ball, or food
treat. Stop and stand still several times throughout the
walk, just as you would when window shopping or
meeting a friend. Use the lure to make sure the dog
slows down and stays close whenever you stop.

When teaching the dog to heel, we generally want
her to sit in heel position when we stop. Teach heel

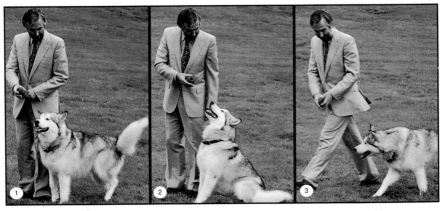

Using a toy to teach sit-heel-sit sequences: 1) "Phoenix, heel!" Standing still, move lure up and back over dog's muzzle.... 2) To position dog sitting in heel position on your left side. 3) "Phoenix, heel!" wagging lure in left hand. Change lure to right hand in preparation for sit signal.

122

position at the standstill and the dog will learn that the default heel position is sitting by your side (left or right—your choice, unless you wish to compete in obedience trials, in which case the dog must heel on the left).

Several times a day, stand up and call your dog to come and sit in heel position—"Fido, heel!" For example, instruct the dog to come to heel each time there are commercials on TV, or each time you turn a page of a novel, and the dog will get it in a single evening.

Practice straight-line heeling and turns separately. With the dog sitting at heel, teach him to turn in place. After each quarter-turn, half-turn or full turn in place, lure the dog to sit at heel. Now it's time for short straight-line heeling sequences, no more than a few steps at a time. Always think of heeling in terms of Sit-Heel-Sit sequences—start and end with the dog in position and do your best to keep him there when moving. Progressively increase the number of steps in each sequence. When the dog remains close for 20 yards of straight line heeling, it is time to add a few turns and then sign up for a happy-heeling obedience class to get some advice from the experts.

4) Use hand signal only to lure dog to sit as you stop. Eventually, dog will sit automatically at heel whenever you stop. 5) "Good dog!"

NO PULLING ON LEASH

You can start teaching your dog not to pull on leash anywhere—in front of the television or outdoors—but regardless of location, you must not take a single step with tension in the leash. For a reason known only to dogs, even just a couple of paces of pulling on leash is intrinsically motivating and diabolically rewarding. Instead, attach the leash to the dog's collar, grasp the other end firmly with both hands held close to your chest, and stand still—do not budge an inch. Have somebody watch you with a stopwatch to time your progress, or else you will never believe this will work and so you will not even try the exercise, and your shoulder and the dog's neck will be traumatized for years to come.

Stand still and wait for the dog to stop pulling, and to sit and/or lie down. All dogs stop pulling and sit eventually. Most take only a couple of minutes; the all-time record is 22 ⅕ minutes. Time how long it takes. Gently praise the dog when he stops pulling, and as soon as he sits, enthusiastically praise the dog and take just one step forwards, then immediately stand still. This single step usually demonstrates the ballistic reinforcing nature of pulling on leash; most dogs explode to the end of the leash, so be prepared for the strain. Stand firm and wait for the dog to sit again. Repeat this half a dozen times and you will probably notice a progressive reduction in the force of the dog's one-step explosions and a radical reduction in the time it takes for the dog to sit each time.

As the dog learns "Sit we go" and "Pull we stop," she will begin to walk forward calmly with each single step and automatically sit when you stop. Now try two steps before you stop. Wooooooo! Scary! When the dog has mastered two steps at a time, try for three. After each success, progressively increase the number of steps in the sequence: try four steps and then six, eight, ten and twenty steps before stopping. Congratulations! You are now walking the dog on leash.

Whenever walking with the dog (off leash or on leash), make sure you stop periodically to practice a few position commands and stays before instructing the dog to "Walk on!" (Remember, you want the dog to be compliant everywhere, not just in the kitchen when his dinner is at hand.) For example, stopping every 25 yards to briefly train the dog amounts to over 200 training interludes within a single three-mile stroll. And each training session is in a different location. You will not believe the improvement within just the first mile of the first walk.

To put it another way, integrating training into a walk offers 200 separate opportunities to use the continuance of the walk as a reward to reinforce the dog's education. Moreover, some training interludes may comprise continuing education for the dog's walking skills: Alternate short periods of the dog walking calmly by your side with periods when the dog is allowed to sniff and investigate the environment. Now sniffing odors on the grass and meeting other dogs become rewards which reinforce the dog's calm and mannerly demeanor. Good Lord! Whatever next? Many enjoyable walks together of course. Happy trails!

THE IMPORTANCE OF TRICKS

Nothing will improve a dog's quality of life better than having a few tricks under its belt. Teaching any trick expands the dog's vocabulary, which facilitates communication and improves the owner's control. Also, specific tricks help prevent and resolve specific behavior problems. For example, by teaching the dog to fetch his toys, the dog learns carrying a toy makes the owner happy and, therefore, will be more likely to chew his toy than other inappropriate items.

More important, teaching tricks prompts owners to lighten up and train with a sunny disposition. Really, tricks should be no different from any other behaviors we put on cue. But they are. When teaching tricks, owners have a much sweeter attitude, which in turn motivates the dog and improves her willingness to comply. The dog feels tricks are a blast, but formal commands are a drag. In fact, tricks are so enjoyable, they may be used as rewards in training by asking the dog to come, sit and down-stay and then rollover for a tummy rub. Go on, try it: Crack a smile and even giggle when the dog promptly and willingly lies down and stays.

Most important, performing tricks prompts onlookers to smile and giggle. Many people are scared of dogs, especially large ones. And nothing can be more off-putting for a dog than to be constantly confronted by strangers who don't like him because of his size or the way he looks. Uneasy people put the dog on edge, causing him to back off and bark, only frightening people all the more. And so a vicious circle develops, with the people's fear fueling the dog's fear *and vice versa*. Instead, tie a pink ribbon to your dog's collar and practice all sorts of tricks on walks and in the park, and you will be pleasantly amazed how it changes people's attitudes toward your friendly dog. The dog's repertoire of tricks is limited only by the trainer's imagination. Below I have described three of my favorites:

SPEAK AND SHUSH

The training sequence involved in teaching a dog to bark on request is no different from that used when training any behavior on cue: request—lure—response—reward. As always, the secret of success lies in finding an effective lure. If the dog always barks at the doorbell, for example, say "Rover, speak!", have an accomplice ring the doorbell, then reward the dog for barking. After a few woofs, ask Rover to "Shush!", waggle a food treat under his nose (to entice him to sniff and thus to shush), praise him when quiet and eventually offer the treat as a reward. Alternate "Speak" and "Shush," progressively increasing the length of shush-time between each barking bout.

PLAYBOW

With the dog standing, say "Bow!" and lower the food lure (palm upwards) to rest between the dog's forepaws. Praise as the dog lowers

her forequarters and sternum to the ground (as when teaching the down), but then lure the dog to stand and offer the treat. On successive trials, gradually increase the length of time the dog is required to remain in the playbow posture in order to gain a food reward. If the dog's rear end collapses into a down, say nothing and offer no reward; simply start over.

BE A BEAR

With the dog sitting backed into a corner to prevent him from toppling over backwards, say "Be a Bear!" With bent paw and palm down, raise a lure upwards and backwards along the top of the dog's muzzle. Praise the dog when he sits up on his haunches and offer the treat as a reward. To prevent the dog from standing on his hind legs, keep the lure closer to the dog's muzzle. On each trial, progressively increase the length of time the dog is required to sit up to receive a food reward. Since lure/ reward training is so easy, teach the dog to stand and walk on his hind legs as well!

Teaching "Be a Bear"

chapter 9

Getting
Active
with your Dog
by Bardi McLennan

Once you and your dog have graduated from basic obedience training and are beginning to work together as a team, you can take part in the growing world of dog activities. There are so many fun things to do with your dog! Just remember, people and dogs don't always learn at the same pace, so don't be upset if you (or your dog) need more than two basic training courses before your team becomes operational. Even smart dogs don't go straight to college from kindergarten!

Just as there are events geared to certain types of dogs, so there are ones that are more appealing to certain types of people. In some

128

activities, you give the commands and your dog does the work (upland game hunting is one example), while in others, such as agility, you'll both get a workout. You may want to aim for prestigious titles to add to your dog's name, or you may want nothing more than the sheer enjoyment of being around other people and their dogs. Passive or active, participation has its own rewards.

Consider your dog's physical capabilities when looking into any of the canine activities. It's easy to see that a Basset Hound is not built for the racetrack, nor would a Chihuahua be the breed of choice for pulling a sled. A loyal dog will attempt almost anything you ask him to do, so it is up to you to know your dog's limitations. A dog must be physically sound in order to compete at any level in athletic activities, and being mentally sound is a definite plus. Advanced age, however, may not be a deterrent. Many dogs still hunt and herd at ten or twelve years of age. It's entirely possible for dogs to be "fit at 50." Take your dog for a checkup, explain to your vet the type of activity you have in mind and be guided by his or her findings.

All dogs seem to love playing flyball.

You needn't be restricted to breed-specific sports if it's only fun you're after. Certain AKC activities are limited to designated breeds; however, as each new trial, test or sport has grown in popularity, so has the variety of breeds encouraged to participate at a fun level.

But don't shortchange your fun, or that of your dog, by thinking only of the basic function of her breed. Once a dog has learned how to learn, she can be taught to do just about anything as long as the size of the dog is right for the job and you both think it is fun and rewarding. In other words, you are a team.

To get involved in any of the activities detailed in this chapter, look for the names and addresses of the organizations that sponsor them in Chapter 13. You can also ask your breeder or a local dog trainer for contacts.

Official American Kennel Club Activities

The following tests and trials are some of the events sanctioned by the AKC and sponsored by various dog clubs. Your dog's expertise will be rewarded with impressive titles. You can participate just for fun, or be competitive and go for those awards.

OBEDIENCE

Training classes begin with pups as young as three months of age in kindergarten puppy training,

You can compete in obedience trials with a well trained dog.

then advance to pre-novice (all exercises on lead) and go on to novice, which is where you'll start off-lead work. In obedience classes dogs learn to sit, stay, heel and come through a variety of exercises. Once you've got the basics down, you can enter obedience trials and work toward earning your dog's first degree, a C.D. (Companion Dog).

The next level is called "Open," in which jumps and retrieves perk up the dog's interest. Passing grades in competition at this level earn a C.D.X. (Companion Dog Excellent). Beyond that lies the goal of the most ambitious—Utility (U.D. and even U.D.X. or OTCh, an Obedience Champion).

AGILITY

All dogs can participate in the latest canine sport to have gained worldwide popularity for its fun and excitement, agility. It began in England as a canine version of horse show-jumping, but because dogs are more agile and able to perform on verbal commands, extra feats were added such as climbing, balancing and racing through tunnels or in and out of weave poles. Many of the obstacles (regulation or homemade) can be set up in your own backyard. If the agility bug bites, you could end up in international competition!

For starters, your dog should be obedience trained, even though, in the beginning, the lessons may all be taught on lead. Once the dog understands the commands (and you do, too), it's as easy as guiding the dog over a prescribed course, one obstacle at a time. In competition, the race is against the clock, so wear your running shoes! The dog starts with 200 points and the judge deducts for infractions and misadventures along the way.

All dogs seem to love agility and respond to it as if they were being turned loose in a playground paradise. Your dog's enthusiasm will be contagious; agility turns into great fun for dog and owner.

FIELD TRIALS AND HUNTING TESTS

There are field trials and hunting tests for the sporting breeds—retrievers, spaniels and pointing breeds, and for some hounds—Bassets, Beagles and Dachshunds. Field trials are competitive events that test a dog's ability to perform the functions for which she was bred. Hunting tests, which are open to retrievers,

---

TITLES AWARDED BY THE AKC

Conformation: Ch. (Champion)

Obedience: CD (Companion Dog); CDX (Companion Dog Excellent); UD (Utility Dog); UDX (Utility Dog Excellent); OTCh. (Obedience Trial Champion)

Field: JH (Junior Hunter); SH (Senior Hunter); MH (Master Hunter); AFCh. (Amateur Field Champion); FCh. (Field Champion)

Lure Coursing: JC (Junior Courser); SC (Senior Courser)

Herding: HT (Herding Tested); PT (Pre-Trial Tested); HS (Herding Started); HI (Herding Intermediate); HX (Herding Excellent); HCh. (Herding Champion)

Tracking: TD (Tracking Dog); TDX (Tracking Dog Excellent)

Agility: NAD (Novice Agility); OAD (Open Agility); ADX (Agility Excellent); MAX (Master Agility)

Earthdog Tests: JE (Junior Earthdog); SE (Senior Earthdog); ME (Master Earthdog)

Canine Good Citizen: CGC

Combination: DC (Dual Champion—Ch. and Fch.); TC (Triple Champion—Ch., Fch., and OTCh.)

---

spaniels and pointing breeds only, are noncompetitive and are a means of judging the dog's ability as well as that of the handler.

Hunting is a very large and complex part of canine sports, and if you own one of the breeds that hunts, the events are a great treat for your dog and you. He gets to do what he was bred for, and you get to work with him and watch him do it. You'll be proud of and amazed at what your dog can do.

Fortunately, the AKC publishes a series of booklets on these events, which outline the rules and regulations and include a glossary of the sometimes complicated terms. The AKC also publishes newsletters for field trialers and hunting test enthusiasts. The United Kennel Club (UKC) also has informative materials for the hunter and his dog.

Retrievers and other sporting breeds get to do what they're bred to in hunting tests.

HERDING TESTS AND TRIALS

Herding, like hunting, dates back to the first known uses man made of dogs. The interest in herding today is widespread, and if you own a herding breed, you can join in the activity. Herding dogs are tested for their natural skills to keep a flock of ducks, sheep or cattle together. If your dog shows potential, you can start at the testing level, where your dog can earn a title for showing an inherent herding ability. With training you can advance to the trial level, where your dog should be capable of controlling even difficult livestock in diverse situations.

LURE COURSING

The AKC Tests and Trials for Lure Coursing are open to traditional sighthounds—Greyhounds, Whippets,

Borzoi, Salukis, Afghan Hounds, Ibizan Hounds and Scottish Deerhounds—as well as to Basenjis and Rhodesian Ridgebacks. Hounds are judged on overall ability, follow, speed, agility and endurance. This is possibly the most exciting of the trials for spectators, because the speed and agility of the dogs is awesome to watch as they chase the lure (or "course") in heats of two or three dogs at a time.

TRACKING

This tracking dog is hot on the trail.

Tracking is another activity in which almost any dog can compete because every dog that sniffs the ground when taken outdoors is, in fact, tracking. The hard part comes when the rules as to what, when and where the dog tracks are determined by a person, not the dog! Tracking tests cover a large area of fields, woods and roads. The tracks are laid hours before the dogs go to work on them, and include "tricks" like cross-tracks and sharp turns. If you're interested in search-and-rescue work, this is the place to start.

EARTHDOG TESTS FOR SMALL TERRIERS AND DACHSHUNDS

These tests are open to Australian, Bedlington, Border, Cairn, Dandie Dinmont, Smooth and Wire Fox, Lakeland, Norfolk, Norwich, Scottish, Sealyham, Skye, Welsh and West Highland White Terriers as well as Dachshunds. The dogs need no prior training for this terrier sport. There is a qualifying test on the day of the event, so dog and handler learn the rules on the spot. These tests, or "digs," sometimes end with informal races in the late afternoon.

133

Here are some of the extracurricular obedience and racing activities that are not regulated by the AKC or UKC, but are generally run by clubs or a group of dog fanciers and are often open to all.

Canine Freestyle This activity is something new on the scene and is variously likened to dancing, dressage or ice skating. It is meant to show the athleticism of the dog, but also requires showmanship on the part of the dog's handler. If you and your dog like to ham it up for friends, you might want to look into freestyle.

Lure coursing lets sighthounds do what they do best—run!

Scent Hurdle Racing Scent hurdle racing is purely a fun activity sponsored by obedience clubs with members forming competing teams. The height of the hurdles is based on the size of the shortest dog on the team. On a signal, one team dog is released on each of two side-by-side courses and must clear every hurdle before picking up its own dumbbell from a platform and returning over the jumps to the handler. As each dog returns, the next on that team is sent. Of course, that is what the dogs are supposed to do. When the dogs improvise (going under or around the hurdles, stealing another dog's dumbbell, and so forth), it no doubt frustrates the handlers, but just adds to the fun for everyone else.

Flyball This type of racing is similar, but after negotiating the four hurdles, the dog comes to a flyball box, steps on a lever that releases a tennis ball into the air, catches the ball and returns over the hurdles to the starting point. This game also becomes extremely fun for spectators because the dogs sometimes cheat by catching a ball released by the dog in the next lane. Three titles can be earned—Flyball Dog (F.D.), Flyball Dog Excellent (F.D.X.) and Flyball Dog Champion (Fb.D.Ch.)—all awarded by the North American Flyball Association, Inc.

Dogsledding The name conjures up the Rocky Mountains or the frigid North, but you can find dogsled clubs in such unlikely spots as Maryland, North Carolina and Virginia! Dogsledding is primarily for the Nordic breeds such as the Alaskan Malamutes, Siberian Huskies and Samoyeds, but other breeds can try. There are some practical backyard applications to this sport, too. With parental supervision, almost any strong dog could pull a child's sled.

Coming over the A-frame on an agility course.

These are just some of the many recreational ways you can get to know and understand your multifaceted dog better and have fun doing it.

chapter 10

Your Dog
and your
Family

by Bardi McLennan

Adding a dog automatically increases your family by one, no matter whether you live alone in an apartment or are part of a mother, father and six kids household. The single-person family is fair game for numerous and varied canine misconceptions as to who is dog and who pays the bills, whereas a dog in a houseful of children will consider himself to be just one of the gang, littermates all. One dog and one child may give a dog reason to believe they are both kids or both dogs. Either interpretation requires parental supervision and sometimes speedy intervention.

As soon as one paw goes through the door into your home, Rufus (or Rufina) has to make many adjustments to become a part of your family. Your job is to make him fit in as painlessly as possible. An older dog may have some frame of reference from past experience, but to a 10-week-old puppy, everything is brand new: people, furniture, stairs, when and where people eat, sleep or watch TV, his own place and everyone else's space, smells, sounds, outdoors—everything!

Puppies, and newly acquired dogs of any age, do not need what we think of as "freedom." If you leave a new dog or puppy loose in the house, you will almost certainly return to chaotic destruction and the dog will forever after equate your homecoming with a time of punishment to be dreaded. It is unfair to give your dog what amounts to "freedom to get into trouble." Instead, confine him to a crate for brief periods of your absence (up to three or four hours) and, for the long haul, a workday for example, confine him to one untrashable area with his own toys, a bowl of water and a radio left on (low) in another room.

Lots of pets get along with each other just fine.

For the first few days, when not confined, put Rufus on a long leash tied to your wrist or waist. This umbilical cord method enables the dog to learn all about you from your body language and voice, and to learn by his own actions which things in the house are NO! and which ones are rewarded by "Good dog." Housetraining will be easier with the pup always by your side. Speaking of which, accidents do happen. That goal of "completely housetrained" takes up to a year, or the length of time it takes the pup to mature.

The All-Adult Family

Most dogs in an adults-only household today are likely to be latchkey pets, with no one home all day but the dog. When you return after a tough day on the job, the dog can and should be your relaxation therapy. But going home can instead be a daily frustration.

Separation anxiety is a very common problem for the dog in a working household. It may begin with whines and barks of loneliness, but it will soon escalate into a frenzied destruction derby. That is why it is so important to set aside the time to teach a dog to relax when left alone in his confined area and to understand that he can trust you to return.

Let the dog get used to your work schedule in easy stages. Confine him to one room and go in and out of that room over and over again. Be casual about it. No physical, voice or eye contact. When the pup no longer even notices your comings and goings, leave the house for varying lengths of time, returning to stay home for a few minutes and gradually increasing the time away. This training can take days, but the dog is learning that you haven't left him forever and that he can trust you.

Any time you leave the dog, but especially during this training period, be casual about your departure. No anxiety-building fond farewells. Just "Bye" and go! Remember the "Good dog" when you return to find everything more or less as you left it.

If things are a mess (or even a disaster) when you return, greet the dog, take him outside to eliminate, and then put him in his crate while you clean up. Rant and rave in the shower! *Do not* punish the dog. You were not there when it happened, and the rule is: Only punish as you catch the dog in the act of wrongdoing. Obviously, it makes sense to get your latchkey puppy when you'll have a week or two to spend on these training essentials.

Family weekend activities should include Rufus whenever possible. Depending on the pup's age, now is the time for a long walk in the park, playtime in the backyard, a hike in the woods. Socializing is as important as health care, good food and physical exercise, so visiting Aunt Emma or Uncle Harry and the next-door neighbor's dog or cat is essential to developing an outgoing, friendly temperament in your pet.

If you are a single adult, socializing Rufus at home and away will prevent him from becoming overly protective of you (or just overly attached) and will also prevent such behavioral problems as dominance or fear of strangers.

Babies

Whether already here or on the way, babies figure larger than life in the eyes of a dog. If the dog is there first, let him in on all your baby preparations in the house. When baby arrives, let Rufus sniff any item of clothing that has been on the baby before Junior comes home. Then let Mom greet the dog first before introducing the new family member. Hold the baby down for the dog to see and sniff, but make sure someone's holding the dog on lead in case of any sudden moves. Don't play keep-away or tease the dog with the baby, which only invites undesirable jumping up.

The dog and the baby are "family," and for starters can be treated almost as equals. Things rapidly change, however, especially when baby takes to creeping around on all fours on the dog's turf or, better yet, has yummy pudding all over her face and hands! That's when a lot of things in the dog's and baby's lives become more separate than equal.

Dogs are perfect confidants.

Toddlers make terrible dog owners, but if you can't avoid the combination, use patient discipline (that is, positive teaching rather than punishment), and use time-outs before you run out of patience.

A dog and a baby (or toddler, or an assertive young child) should never be left alone together. Take the dog with you or confine him. With a baby or youngsters in the house, you'll have plenty of use for that wonderful canine safety device called a crate!

Young Children

Any dog in a house with kids will behave pretty much as the kids do, good or bad. But even good dogs and good children can get into trouble when play becomes rowdy and active.

Teach children how to play nicely with a puppy.

Legs bobbing up and down, shrill voices screeching, a ball hurtling overhead, all add up to exuberant frustration for a dog who's just trying to be part of the gang. In a pack of puppies, any legs or toys being chased would be caught by a set of teeth, and all the pups involved would understand that is how the game is played. Kids do not understand this, nor do parents tolerate it. Bring Rufus indoors before you have reason to regret it. This is time-out, not a punishment.

You can explain the situation to the children and tell them they must play quieter games until the puppy learns not to grab them with his mouth. Unfortunately, you can't explain it that easily to the dog. With adult supervision, they will learn how to play together.

Young children love to tease. Sticking their faces or wiggling their hands or fingers in the dog's face is teasing. To another person it might be just annoying, but it is threatening to a dog. There's another difference: We can make the child stop by an explanation, but the only way a dog can stop it is with a warning growl and then with teeth. Teasing is the major cause of children being bitten by their pets. Treat it seriously.

Older Children

The best age for a child to get a first dog is between the ages of 8 and 12. That's when kids are able to accept some real responsibility for their pet. Even so, take the child's vow of "I will never *ever* forget to feed (brush, walk, etc.) the dog" for what it's worth: a child's good intention at that moment. Most kids today have extra lessons, soccer practice, Little League, ballet, and so forth piled on top of school schedules. There will be many times when Mom will have to come to the dog's rescue. "I walked the dog for you so you can set the table for me" is one way to get around a missed appointment without laying on blame or guilt.

Kids in this age group make excellent obedience train ers because they are into the teaching/learning process themselves and they lack the self-consciousness of adults. Attending a dog show is something the whole family can enjoy, and watching Junior Showmanship may catch the eye of the kids. Older children can begin to get involved in many of the recreational activities that were reviewed in the previous chapter. Some of the agility obstacles, for example, can be set up in the backyard as a family project (with an adult making sure all the equipment is safe and secure for the dog).

Older kids are also beginning to look to the future, and may envision themselves as veterinarians or trainers or show dog handlers or writers of the next Lassie best-seller. Dogs are perfect confidants for these dreams. They won't tell a soul.

Other Pets

Introduce all pets tactfully. In a dog/cat situation, hold the dog, not the cat. Let two dogs meet on neutral turf—a stroll in the park or a walk down the street—with both on loose leads to permit all the normal canine ways of saying hello, including routine sniffing, circling, more sniffing, and so on. Small creatures such as hamsters, chinchillas or mice must be kept safe from their natural predators (dogs and cats).

Festive Family Occasions

Parties are great for people, but not necessarily for puppies. Until all the guests have arrived, put the dog in his crate or in a room where he won't be disturbed. A socialized dog can join the fun later as long as he's not underfoot, annoying guests or into the hors d'oeuvres.

There are a few dangers to consider, too. Doors opening and closing can allow a puppy to slip out unnoticed in the confusion, and you'll be organizing a search party instead of playing host or hostess. Party food and buffet service are not for dogs. Let Rufus party in his crate with a nice big dog biscuit.

At Christmas time, not only are tree decorations dangerous and breakable (and perhaps family heirlooms), but extreme caution should be taken with the lights, cords and outlets for the tree lights and any other festive lighting. Occasionally a dog lifts a leg, ignoring the fact that the tree is indoors. To avoid this, use a canine repellent, made for gardens, on the tree. Or keep him out of the tree room unless supervised. And whatever you do, *don't* invite trouble by hanging his toys on the tree!

Car Travel

Before you plan a vacation by car or RV with Rufus, be sure he enjoys car travel. Nothing spoils a holiday quicker than a carsick dog! Work within the dog's comfort level. Get in the car with the dog in his crate or attached to a canine car safety belt and just sit there until he relaxes. That's all. Next time, get in the car, turn on the engine and go nowhere. Just sit. When that is okay, turn on the engine and go around the block. Now you can go for a ride and include a stop where you get out, leaving the dog for a minute or two.

On a warm day, always park in the shade and leave windows open several inches. And return quickly. It only takes 10 minutes for a car to become an overheated steel death trap.

Motel or Pet Motel?

Not all motels or hotels accept pets, but you have a much better choice today than even a few years ago. To find a dog-friendly lodging, look at *On the Road Again With Man's Best Friend*, a series of directories that detail bed and breakfasts, inns, family resorts and other hotels/motels. Some places require a refundable deposit to cover any damage incurred by the dog. More B&Bs accept pets now, but some restrict the size.

If taking Rufus with you is not feasible, check out boarding kennels in your area. Your veterinarian may offer this service, or recommend a kennel or two he or she is familiar with. Go see the facilities for yourself, ask about exercise, diet, housing, and so on. Or, if you'd rather have Rufus stay home, look into bonded petsitters, many of whom will also bring in the mail and water your plants.

chapter 11

Your Dog
and your
Community

by Bardi McLennan

Step outside your home with your dog and you are no longer just family, you are both part of your community. This is when the phrase "responsible pet ownership" takes on serious implications. For starters, it means you pick up after your dog—not just occasionally, but every time your dog eliminates away from home. That means you have joined the Plastic Baggy Brigade! You always have plastic sandwich bags in your pocket and several in the car. It means you teach your kids how to use them, too. If you think this is "yucky," just imagine what the person (a non-doggy person) who inadvertently steps in the mess thinks!

Your responsibility extends to your neighbors: To their ears (no annoying barking); to their property (their garbage, their lawn, their flower beds, their cat—especially their cat); to their kids (on bikes, at play); to their kids' toys and sports equipment.

There are numerous dog-related laws, ranging from simple dog licensing and leash laws to those holding you liable for any physical injury or property damage done by your dog. These laws are in place to protect everyone in the community, including you and your dog. There are town ordinances and state laws which are by no means the same in all towns or all states. Ignorance of the law won't get you off the hook. The time to find out what the laws are where you live is now.

Be sure your dog's license is current. This is not just a good local ordinance, it can make the difference between finding your lost dog or not.

Dressing your dog up makes him appealing to strangers.

Many states now require proof of rabies vaccination and that the dog has been spayed or neutered before issuing a license. At the same time, keep up the dog's annual immunizations.

Never let your dog run loose in the neighborhood. This will not only keep you on the right side of the leash law, it's the outdoor version of the rule about not giving your dog "freedom to get into trouble."

Good Canine Citizen

Sometimes it's hard for a dog's owner to assess whether or not the dog is sufficiently socialized to be accepted by the community at large. Does Rufus or Rufina display good, controlled behavior in public? The AKC's Canine Good Citizen program is available through many dog organizations. If your dog passes the test, the title "CGC" is earned.

The overall purpose is to turn your dog into a good neighbor and to teach you about your responsibility to your community as a dog owner. Here are the ten things your dog must do willingly:

1. Accept a stranger stopping to chat with you.
2. Sit and be petted by a stranger.
3. Allow a stranger to handle him or her as a groomer or veterinarian would.
4. Walk nicely on a loose lead.
5. Walk calmly through a crowd.
6. Sit and down on command, then stay in a sit or down position while you walk away.
7. Come when called.
8. Casually greet another dog.
9. React confidently to distractions.
10. Accept being left alone with someone other than you and not become overly agitated or nervous.

Schools and Dogs

Schools are getting involved with pet ownership on an educational level. It has been proven that children who are kind to animals are humane in their attitude toward other people as adults.

A dog is a child's best friend, and so children are often primary pet owners, if not the primary caregivers. Unfortunately, they are also the ones most often bitten by dogs. This occurs due to a lack of understanding that pets, no matter how sweet, cuddly and loving, are still animals. Schools, along with parents, dog clubs, dog fanciers and the AKC, are working to change all that with video programs for children not only in grade school, but in the nursery school and pre-kindergarten age group. Teaching youngsters how to be responsible dog owners is important community work. When your dog has a CGC, volunteer to take part in an educational classroom event put on by your dog club.

Boy Scout Merit Badge

A Merit Badge for Dog Care can be earned by any Boy Scout ages 11 to 18. The requirements are not easy, but amount to a complete course in responsible dog care and general ownership. Here are just a few of the things a Scout must do to earn that badge:

> Point out ten parts of the dog using the correct names.

> Give a report (signed by parent or guardian) on your care of the dog (feeding, food used, housing, exercising, grooming and bathing), plus what has been done to keep the dog healthy.

> Explain the right way to obedience train a dog, and demonstrate three comments.

> Several of the requirements have to do with health care, including first aid, handling a hurt dog, and the dangers of home treatment for a serious ailment.

> The final requirement is to know the local laws and ordinances involving dogs.

There are similar programs for Girl Scouts and 4-H members.

Local Clubs

Local dog clubs are no longer in existence just to put on a yearly dog show. Today, they are apt to be the hub of the community's involvement with pets. Dog clubs conduct educational forums with big-name speakers, stage demonstrations of canine talent in a busy mall and take dogs of various breeds to schools for class-room discussion.

The quickest way to feel accepted as a member in a club is to volunteer your services! Offer to help with something—anything—and watch your popularity (and your interest) grow.

Therapy Dogs

Once your dog has earned that essential CGC and reliably demonstrates a steady, calm temperament, you could look into what therapy dogs are doing in your area.

Therapy dogs go with their owners to visit patients at hospitals or nursing homes, generally remaining on leash but able to coax a pat from a stiffened hand, a smile from a blank face, a few words from sealed lips or a hug from someone in need of love.

Nursing homes cover a wide range of patient care. Some specialize in care of the elderly, some in the treatment of specific illnesses, some in physical therapy. Children's facilities also welcome visits from trained therapy dogs for boosting morale in their pediatric patients. Hospice care for the terminally ill and the at-home care of AIDS patients are other areas where this canine visiting is desperately needed. Therapy dog training comes first.

Your dog can make a difference in lots of lives.

There is a lot more involved than just taking your nice friendly pooch to someone's bedside. Doing therapy dog work involves your own emotional stability as well as that of your dog. But once you have met all the requirements for this work, making the rounds once a week or once a month with your therapy dog is possibly the most rewarding of all community activities.

Disaster Aid

This community service is definitely not for everyone, partly because it is time-consuming. The initial training is rigorous, and there can be no let-up in the continuing workouts, because members are on call 24 hours a day to go wherever they are needed at a moment's notice. But if you think you would like to be able to assist in a disaster, look into search-and-rescue work. The network of search-and-rescue volunteers is worldwide, and all members of the American Rescue Dog Association (ARDA) who are qualified to do this work are volunteers who train and maintain their own dogs.

Physical Aid

Most people are familiar with Seeing Eye dogs, which serve as blind people's eyes, but not with all the other work that dogs are trained to do to assist the disabled. Dogs are also specially trained to pull wheelchairs, carry school books, pick up dropped objects, open and close doors. Some also are ears for the deaf. All these assistance-trained dogs, by the way, are allowed anywhere "No Pet" signs exist (as are therapy dogs when

Making the rounds with your therapy dog can be very rewarding.

properly identified). Getting started in any of this fascinating work requires a background in dog training and canine behavior, but there are also volunteer jobs ranging from answering the phone to cleaning out kennels to providing a foster home for a puppy. You have only to ask.

part four

Beyond the Basics

chapter 12

Recommended Reading

Books

ABOUT HEALTH CARE

Ackerman, Lowell. *Guide to Skin and Haircoat Problems in Dogs.* Loveland, Colo.: Alpine Publications, 1994.

Alderton, David. *The Dog Care Manual.* Hauppauge, N.Y.: Barron's Educational Series, Inc., 1986.

American Kennel Club. *American Kennel Club Dog Care and Training.* New York: Howell Book House, 1991.

Bamberger, Michelle, DVM. *Help! The Quick Guide to First Aid for Your Dog.* New York: Howell Book House, 1995.

Carlson, Delbert, DVM, and James Giffin, MD. *Dog Owner's Home Veterinary Handbook.* New York: Howell Book House, 1992.

DeBitetto, James, DVM, and Sarah Hodgson. *You & Your Puppy.* New York: Howell Book House, 1995.

Humphries, Jim, DVM. *Dr. Jim's Animal Clinic for Dogs.* New York: Howell Book House, 1994.

McGinnis, Terri. *The Well Dog Book.* New York: Random House, 1991.

Pitcairn, Richard and Susan. *Natural Health for Dogs.* Emmaus, Pa.: Rodale Press, 1982.

ABOUT DOG SHOWS

Hall, Lynn. *Dog Showing for Beginners.* New York: Howell Book House, 1994.

Nichols, Virginia Tuck. *How to Show Your Own Dog.* Neptune, N. J.: TFH, 1970.

Vanacore, Connie. *Dog Showing, An Owner's Guide.* New York: Howell Book House, 1990.

ABOUT TRAINING

Ammen, Amy. *Training in No Time.* New York: Howell Book House, 1995.

Baer, Ted. *Communicating With Your Dog.* Hauppauge, N.Y.: Barron's Educational Series, Inc., 1989.

Benjamin, Carol Lea. *Dog Problems.* New York: Howell Book House, 1989.

Benjamin, Carol Lea. *Dog Training for Kids.* New York: Howell Book House, 1988.

Benjamin, Carol Lea. *Mother Knows Best.* New York: Howell Book House, 1985.

Benjamin, Carol Lea. *Surviving Your Dog's Adolescence.* New York: Howell Book House, 1993.

Bohnenkamp, Gwen. *Manners for the Modern Dog.* San Francisco: Perfect Paws, 1990.

Dibra, Bashkim. *Dog Training by Bash.* New York: Dell, 1992.

Dunbar, Ian, PhD, MRCVS. *Dr. Dunbar's Good Little Dog Book,* James & Kenneth Publishers, 2140 Shattuck Ave. #2406, Berkeley, Calif. 94704. (510) 658–8588. Order from the publisher.

Dunbar, Ian, PhD, MRCVS. *How to Teach a New Dog Old Tricks,* James & Kenneth Publishers. Order from the publisher; address above.

Dunbar, Ian, PhD, MRCVS, and Gwen Bohnenkamp. Booklets on *Preventing Aggression; Housetraining; Chewing; Digging; Barking; Socialization; Fearfulness; and Fighting,* James & Kenneth Publishers. Order from the publisher; address above.

Evans, Job Michael. *People, Pooches and Problems.* New York: Howell Book House, 1991.

Kilcommons, Brian and Sarah Wilson. *Good Owners, Great Dogs.* New York: Warner Books, 1992.

McMains, Joel M. *Dog Logic—Companion Obedience.* New York: Howell Book House, 1992.

Rutherford, Clarice and David H. Neil, MRCVS. *How to Raise a Puppy You Can Live With.* Loveland, Colo.: Alpine Publications, 1982.

Volhard, Jack and Melissa Bartlett. *What All Good Dogs Should Know: The Sensible Way to Train.* New York: Howell Book House, 1991.

ABOUT BREEDING

Harris, Beth J. Finder. *Breeding a Litter, The Complete Book of Prenatal and Postnatal Care.* New York: Howell Book House, 1983.

Holst, Phyllis, DVM. *Canine Reproduction.* Loveland, Colo.: Alpine Publications, 1985.

Walkowicz, Chris and Bonnie Wilcox, DVM. *Successful Dog Breeding, The Complete Handbook of Canine Midwifery.* New York: Howell Book House, 1994.

ABOUT ACTIVITIES

American Rescue Dog Association. *Search and Rescue Dogs.* New York: Howell Book House, 1991.

Barwig, Susan and Stewart Hilliard. *Schutzhund.* New York: Howell Book House, 1991.

Beaman, Arthur S. *Lure Coursing.* New York: Howell Book House, 1994.

Daniels, Julie. *Enjoying Dog Agility—From Backyard to Competition.* New York: Doral Publishing, 1990.

Davis, Kathy Diamond. *Therapy Dogs.* New York: Howell Book House, 1992.

Gallup, Davis Anne. *Running With Man's Best Friend.* Loveland, Colo.: Alpine Publications, 1986.

Habgood, Dawn and Robert. *On the Road Again With Man's Best Friend.* New England, Mid-Atlantic, West Coast and Southeast editions. Selective guides to area bed and breakfasts, inns, hotels and resorts that welcome guests and their dogs. New York: Howell Book House, 1995.

Holland, Vergil S. *Herding Dogs.* New York: Howell Book House, 1994.

LaBelle, Charlene G. *Backpacking With Your Dog.* Loveland, Colo.: Alpine Publications, 1993.

Simmons Moake, Jane. *Agility Training, The Fun Sport for All Dogs.* New York: Howell Book House, 1991.

Spencer, James B. *Hup! Training Flushing Spaniels the American Way.* New York: Howell Book House, 1992.

Spencer, James B. *Point! Training the All-Seasons Birddog.* New York: Howell Book House, 1995.

Tarrant, Bill. *Training the Hunting Retriever.* New York: Howell Book House, 1991.

Volhard, Jack and Wendy. *The Canine Good Citizen.* New York: Howell Book House, 1994.

General Titles

Haggerty, Captain Arthur J. *How to Get Your Pet Into Show Business.* New York: Howell Book House, 1994.

McLennan, Bardi. *Dogs and Kids, Parenting Tips.* New York: Howell Book House, 1993.

Moran, Patti J. *Pet Sitting for Profit, A Complete Manual for Professional Success.* New York: Howell Book House, 1992.

Scalisi, Danny and Libby Moses. *When Rover Just Won't Do, Over 2,000 Suggestions for Naming Your Dog.* New York: Howell Book House, 1993.

Sife, Wallace, PhD. *The Loss of a Pet.* New York: Howell Book House, 1993.

Wrede, Barbara J. *Civilizing Your Puppy.* Hauppauge, N.Y.: Barron's Educational Series, 1992.

Magazines

The AKC GAZETTE, The Official Journal for the Sport of Purebred Dogs. American Kennel Club, 51 Madison Ave., New York, NY.

Bloodlines Journal. United Kennel Club, 100 E. Kilgore Rd., Kalamazoo, MI.

Dog Fancy. Fancy Publications, 3 Burroughs, Irvine, CA 92718

Dog World. Maclean Hunter Publishing Corp., 29 N. Wacker Dr., Chicago, IL 60606.

Videos

"SIRIUS Puppy Training," by Ian Dunbar, PhD, MRCVS. James & Kenneth Publishers, 2140 Shattuck Ave. #2406, Berkeley, CA 94704. Order from the publisher.

"Training the Companion Dog," from Dr. Dunbar's British TV Series, James & Kenneth Publishers. (See address above).

The American Kennel Club produces videos on every breed of dog, as well as on hunting tests, field trials and other areas of interest to purebred dog owners. For more information, write to AKC/Video Fulfillment, 5580 Centerview Dr., Suite 200, Raleigh, NC 27606.

chapter 13

Resources

Breed Clubs

Every breed recognized by the American Kennel Club has a national (parent) club. National clubs are a great source of information on your breed. You can get the name of the secretary of the club by contacting:

The American Kennel Club
51 Madison Avenue
New York, NY 10010
(212) 696-8200

There are also numerous all-breed, individual breed, obedience, hunting and other special-interest dog clubs across the country. The American Kennel Club can provide you with a geographical list of clubs to find ones in your area. Contact them at the above address.

Registry Organizations

Registry organizations register purebred dogs. The American Kennel Club is the oldest and largest in this country, and currently recognizes over 130 breeds. The United Kennel Club registers some breeds the AKC doesn't (including the American Pit Bull Terrier and the Miniature Fox Terrier) as well as many of the same breeds. The others included here are for your reference; the AKC can provide you with a list of foreign registries.

American Kennel Club
51 Madison Avenue
New York, NY 10010

United Kennel Club (UKC)
100 E. Kilgore Road
Kalamazoo, MI 49001-5598

American Dog Breeders Assn.
P.O. Box 1771
Salt Lake City, UT 84110
(Registers American Pit Bull Terriers)

Canadian Kennel Club
89 Skyway Avenue
Etobicoke, Ontario
Canada M9W 6R4

National Stock Dog Registry
P.O. Box 402
Butler, IN 46721
(Registers working stock dogs)

Orthopedic Foundation for Animals (OFA)
2300 E. Nifong Blvd.
Columbia, MO 65201-3856
(Hip registry)

Activity Clubs

Write to these organizations for information on the
activities they sponsor.

American Kennel Club
51 Madison Avenue
New York, NY 10010
(Conformation Shows, Obedience Trials, Field
Trials and Hunting Tests, Agility, Canine Good

Citizen, Lure Coursing, Herding, Tracking,
Earthdog Tests, Coonhunting.)

United Kennel Club
100 E. Kilgore Road
Kalamazoo, MI 49001-5598
(Conformation Shows, Obedience Trials, Agility,
Hunting for Various Breeds, Terrier Trials and
more.)

North American Flyball Assn.
1342 Jeff St.
Ypsilanti, MI 48198

International Sled Dog Racing Assn.
P.O. Box 446
Norman, ID 83848-0446

North American Working Dog Assn., Inc.
Southeast Kreisgruppe
P.O. Box 833
Brunswick, GA 31521

Trainers

Association of Pet Dog Trainers
P.O. Box 3734
Salinas, CA 93912
(408) 663-9257

American Dog Trainers' Network
161 West 4th St.
New York, NY 10014
(212) 727-7257

**National Association of Dog Obedience
Instructors**
2286 East Steel Rd.
St. Johns, MI 48879

Associations

American Dog Owners Assn.
1654 Columbia Tpk.
Castleton, NY 12033
(Combats anti-dog legislation)

Delta Society
P.O. Box 1080
Renton, WA 98057-1080
(Promotes the human/animal bond through
pet-assisted therapy and other programs)

Dog Writers Assn. of America (DWAA)
Sally Cooper, Secy.
222 Woodchuck Ln.
Harwinton, CT 06791

National Assn. for Search and Rescue (NASAR)
P.O. Box 3709
Fairfax, VA 22038

Therapy Dogs International
6 Hilltop Road
Mendham, NJ 07945